Labor-Management Cooperation

New Partnerships or Going in Circles?

William N. Cooke
Wayne State University

1990

W.E. UPJOHN INSTITUTE for Employment Research
Kalamazoo, Michigan

Library of Congress Cataloging-in-Publication Data

Cooke, William N.
    Labor-management cooperation : new partnerships or going in
circles? / William N. Cooke.
        p.   cm.
    Includes bibliographical references and index.
        ISBN 0-88099-099-6 (hardcover : acid-free). — ISBN 0-88099-100-3
    (paper : acid-free)
        1. Industrial relations—United States. I. Title.
    HD8072.5.C67 1990
    331'.0973—dc20   90-46159
                                                                                                    CIP

HD
8072.5
.C67
1990
155475
ap. 1992

THE INSTITUTE, a nonprofit research organization, was established on July 1, 1945.
It is an activity of the W. E. Upjohn Unemployment Trustee Corporation, which was
formed in 1932 to administer a fund set aside by the late Dr. W. E. Upjohn for the
purpose of carrying on "research into the causes and effects of unemployment and
measures for the alleviation of unemployment."

The facts presented in this study and the observations and viewpoints expressed are
the sole responsibility of the author. They do not necessarily represent positions of
the W. E. Upjohn Institute for Employment Research.

Cover design by J.R. Underhill.
Index prepared by Shirley Kessel.
Printed in the United States of America.

To Lynn P. Cooke, a hard-nosed critic
with a disarming smile, who has shown me the cost
of confrontation and the benefit of cooperation.

The Author

William Cooke is Professor and Associate Dean for Research in the College of Urban, Labor, and Metropolitan Affairs at Wayne State University. He has been an Associate Professor in the School of Business at the University of Michigan and in the School of Management at Purdue University. Professor Cooke has also been a visiting fellow at Cornell University and a visiting scholar at the University of California, Berkeley. He received his Ph.D. in labor and industrial relations from the University of Illinois in 1977.

He is the author of *Union Organizing and Public Policy: Failure to Negotiate First Contracts* (Upjohn Institute for Employment Research, 1985) and has published extensively in the *Industrial and Labor Relations Review* and in *Industrial Relations* on the topics of union organizing, labor law and NLRB decisionmaking, and union-management cooperation.

Professor Cooke has been an academic advisor and instructor in the UAW-Ford Joint Labor-Management Studies Leadership Program and an instructor in the UAW-GM National Paid Educational Leave Program. He has also been the faculty director of "Strategic Collective Bargaining" and "Negotiating and Administering the Labor Contract" executive education programs at the University of Michigan.

Professor Cooke is currently conducting research on cooperation and union effectiveness, on workplace innovations in union and nonunion organizations, and on the linkages between the workplace and broader societal issues associated with family, education, and substance abuse.

Acknowledgments

Many acknowledgments are due. First, I must thank the hundreds of plant managers, local union officers, and company executives who responded to my surveys. Although I am sure they anticipated seeing the results of these inquiries much earlier, nonetheless I hope what they find herein will be of timely value. Without the excellent research assistance of Lynn Cooke and Melinda Laubscher, the data might never have been collected and assimilated. John Zalusky (AFL-CIO) provided valuable assistance in soliciting responses to my survey of local union officers.

Dave Meyer (University of Akron) provided essential assistance in pulling together diverse secondary data sources and became a coauthor of analyses of company headquarters data, a cooperative effort that has led to richer analyses than could have been accomplished otherwise. Long hours of spirited discussion and debate with Sue Schurman (University of Michigan) about union-management relations have undeniably shaped many points of view expressed in the study. Although I won't hold her accountable for any views expressed, neither do I want to minimize her contribution.

Lynn Cooke (r & i associates), Jack Fiorito (University of Iowa), Doug Fraser (Wayne State University), Allan Hunt (Upjohn Institute for Employment Research), John Stepp (Bill Usery and Associates), and George Strauss (University of California, Berkeley) provided valuable criticism and comment at various stages of this research project. Joan Walker patiently kept retyping and replotting diagrams and charts as the chapters went through what must have appeared as endless revisions.

Finally, through a wide range of labor and management workshops and conferences, I have received valuable and extensive comment from hundreds of managers and union officers. I thank them for helping me look more realistically into the black boxes of empirical research and for their unrelenting insistance on making the reporting of research more accessible and meaningful to those searching for answers in an especially challenging era.

To all of the above, my genuine appreciation.

Foreword

Bill Cooke provides the most thorough examination to date of the potential benefits and costs of labor-management cooperation and factors that influence these potential benefits and costs. Recognizing that both labor and management must derive greater net benefit from cooperation than either party can derive from strictly confrontational relationships, he critically examines why some joint efforts succeed and others fail.

It is fundamentally clear from his analysis that labor-management cooperation requires high levels of mutual respect and trust. It is along these lines that Cooke tackles the overriding problem of how to sustain trust, commitment, and enthusiasm for cooperation. Most writers on this subject conclude that it is most difficult, if not impossible, to sustain these programs in the long term. Unlike most writers, however, Cooke offers a set of specific recommendations to avoid this pitfall and sustain the benefits to both labor and management on a continuing basis. These recommendations, which include establishing labor's claim to its stake in business decisions and performance gains, are worthy of careful consideration.

Cooke provides a critical and balanced view of labor-management cooperation. As such, the evidence and opinions provided are important reading for both union and business leaders. Unions and employers who have either already embarked on cooperative strategies or who are considering entering into cooperative relationships should read this book. Although it is doubtful that this book will be widely read by antiunion executives and managers, I wish it could be required reading for them. Perhaps they would learn that workplace efficiency and workplace democracy are not only compatible, they are essential to American competitiveness in a global marketplace.

Douglas Fraser
Former President of the UAW
and University Professor, Wayne State University

Contents

1

Cooperation

Trying To Make It Work In America

As we enter the 1990s, there can be little doubt that global and domestic nonunion competition have severely challenged traditional collective bargaining relationships in American industry. The market forces brought to bear on industry in the late 1970s and throughout the 1980s have led to important strategic choices by employers and unions, some adversarial and some cooperative. These choices may depict, on one hand, what some observers have called nothing less than the "transformation of American industrial relations" (Kochan, Katz, and McKersie 1986), or what others, on the other hand, view as "nothing new under the sun" (Dunlop 1986). Whether one views ongoing changes as "nothing new" or "a transformation," there are currently unprecedented widespread efforts at joint union-management activities designed to improve labor-management relations and company performance. Do these innovative joint activities, however, hallmark a shift away from historically adversarial relationships between unions and employers? Are industry and union leaders truly pioneering new and lasting partnerships, or are they merely going in circles, buying time and destined to return to a long tradition of adversarial relationships?

This study examines that fundamental question, although any definitive answer at this time would be premature. The purpose of the study is to explore issues regarding the decision to cooperate, the success of cooperative efforts, and the problems that undermine these efforts. The analyses presented are based on a variety of secondary data sources, as well as data from nationwide surveys of plant managers, their local union leader counterparts, and executives of companies parent to the plants sampled.

This first chapter reviews the existing literature and sets the stage for the analyses that follow. Chapter 2 develops a general theoretical framework, which broadly guides the subsequent analyses. Chapter 3 describes companywide labor relations strategies that have recently emerged and examines why some parties have embarked on cooperative relations and why just as many have not. In addition, the objectives and structure of joint programs, as reported by a sample of plant managers and local union leaders, are described. Chapter 4 examines how effective these joint efforts have been and identifies factors that appear to enhance or diminish their effectiveness. Chapter 5 addresses the underlying problems arising in the joint decisionmaking process that undermine the potential success and longevity of cooperative efforts. Finally, how the parties can go about resolving, avoiding, or minimizing the costly effects of these key problems is addressed in chapter 6. In that final chapter, implications for the union movement are also assessed.

I have chosen to avoid reporting many of the statistical details of my analyses. My purpose in doing so is to reach out to a wide audience of local and national union leaders, plant managers and company executives, and various policy makers wrestling with the issues at hand in practical ways. Although this wider audience needs and seeks information and analyses that go beyond the wealth of reported case studies, reports, and testimonials, their interests are not in studying more academic methodological details and nuances of statistical modeling. Where I report the results of various statistical estimations, I have nevertheless adhered strictly to the results and hypothesized cause-effect relations. For readers especially interested in statistical details of the analyses, selected tables reporting the measurement and estimation of pertinent equations are provided in appendices to chapters 3 and 4. Nearly all the statistical estimations used in this study, furthermore, have been published recently or are in press in academic journals and hence available to the interested reader.

Review and Synthesis of the Literature

The literature on cooperation has grown rapidly in recent years, addressing both American and foreign experiences. Nearly all this literature is founded on single company and union case studies, reports, and testimonials. Recognizing that a detailed review of the literature is far beyond the intended scope of this study and that my specific purpose is to examine American industry experiences, I restrict my review to first providing a note on the limited early American experiments and, second, to a general synthesis of the reported potential benefits, costs, and problems associated with American cooperative activities. The review is further restricted to cooperative efforts between union representatives and plant management that (a) are outside traditional contract negotiations and contract administration; (b) contain formalized mechanisms for input from union representatives and/or the employees they represent into management decisions; and (c) are intended to improve company performance at the plant, either through direct efforts aimed at improving productivity, quality, efficiency, etc., and/or through indirect efforts aimed at improving employee well-being, job satisfaction, and/ or the labor-management relations climate.

Excluded, then, are cooperative problemsolving activities that might normally occur during the negotiation and the day-to-day administration of contracts. Although joint programs in health and safety, substance abuse, apprenticeship training, and many others can be seen as contributing to company performance and employee welfare, they are excluded from the present analysis. Their specific foci and restricted activities fall at the periphery of the present investigation and warrant separate analyses. Also excluded are joint activities undertaken outside the plant or company, such as involvement in industry or communitywide joint activities or instances where the parties seek in concert to obtain trade protection from foreign competitors.

Except for labor-management committees, most joint activities are structured to elicit shop-floor participation. These programs, moreover, are very similar in structure and activity, regardless of program title. They revolve around team or group activities in which hourly and salaried employees put their heads together on a fairly regular basis. Their charge is to identify problems and opportunities for improvements in the workplace and, in turn, to develop plans for resolving problems or making improvements. Quality of Work Life (QWL) or Employee

Involvement (EI) programs do not differ substantially from quality circles, work teams, or employee involvement associated with gainsharing arrangements. The programs all appear to tackle issues surrounding productivity, product quality, efficiency, etc., and employee concerns about the work environment, the climate of labor-management relations, and overall job security. Most of these programs also have steering committees involving union officials, most restrict activities to subjects not governed by the labor contract, most are voluntary, and most provide training for team members.

These structural similarities do not imply that there are no differences among the team-based programs. The differences, however, have less to do with structure and purpose and more to do with: (a) the intensity of activity (e.g., the proportion of employees engaged in the activity, frequency of group meetings, the amount of team member training, and the extent of other joint programs); (b) the degree of emphasis placed on selected performance-related factors (quality, productivity, absenteeism, etc.); (c) the amount of autonomy and decisionmaking authority granted to teams; (d) the degree of union leader input (both in the design and facilitation of programs); and (e) whether or not there are financial incentives, either tied directly (i.e. gainsharing) or indirectly (i.e. profit sharing and stock ownership) to employee participation.

In spite of an extensive literature addressing cooperation, there are only a few surveys that begin to document the extent to which cooperative activities have been undertaken. My 1986 nationwide survey of 350 relatively large unionized manufacturing plants (described in chapter 3) indicates that roughly 50 percent have established formalized joint programs of the kind described above. A 1983 Conference Board survey of approximately 400 large companies shows that 56 percent of unionized business units have established programs wherein "employees meet in small groups to discuss production and quality" (Kochan, McKersie, Chalykoff 1986). A 1983-1984 survey of approximately 350 unionized firms in Wisconsin shows that roughly 60 percent have established either shop-floor teams or joint committees (Voos 1987). A 1987 nationwide survey of approximately 150 unionized business units shows that about 50 percent have established "employee participation initiatives"

(Delaney, Ichniowski, and Lewin 1988). Although these various surveys are not fully comparable due to differences in sampling, response rates, and definitions of cooperative activities, they do encompass the most extensive efforts to date at documentation of cooperative efforts. Taken together, these surveys indicate that roughly half of unionized private sector establishments have embarked on cooperative efforts of the nature to be examined by this investigation.

The fact that cooperation between unions and employers is occurring is (in Dunlop's words) nothing new under the sun. Cooperative efforts to improve productivity and production standards were undertaken in the 1920s and afterwards, especially in the railroad, textile, and garment industries (Slichter 1941; Slichter, Healy, and Livernash 1960; Jacoby 1983). Pressured by the War Labor Board during WWII, unions and employers established thousands of joint productivity committees (de Schweinitz 1949). Throughout the post-WWII period, there also were a number of highly publicized but fairly isolated cooperative efforts undertaken; for example, by the Tennessee Valley Authority and the Tennessee Valley Trades and Labor Council, Rushton Coal Mine and the United Mine Workers, and Harmon International and the United Auto Workers (Slichter, Healy, and Livernash 1960; Cammann, Lawler, Ledford, and Seashore 1985). History shows, however, that case after case of these uncommon cooperative committee and team efforts were short-lived.

Even though American union-management cooperative efforts designed to improve company performance and labor-management relations are nothing new, the fact that these efforts are currently widespread is unprecedented. Were these efforts to become central and lasting institutional arrangements of successful collective bargaining relationships, then in the words of Kochan et al., American industrial relations would be transformed. For cooperative efforts to become lasting forms of partnership, however, it must ultimately be demonstrated that the gains to cooperation are greater than the costs and that the net gains at least match those derivable from more traditional or highly adversarial relationships.

There is a rich descriptive literature that identifies a wide range of these potential benefits and costs to management, employees, and union leaders. The literature also identifies several general or recurring problems (e.g., insufficient trust and commitment) that appear to increase specific costs associated with cooperation. Except for discussing these general problems, the literature is largely silent, nonetheless, with respect to identifying salient factors that affect potential benefits and costs, and, consequently, affect the success of cooperative efforts. One of the primary purposes of the present study is to begin filling that void.

Potential Benefits and Costs of Cooperation

Potential benefits and costs associated with cooperation must be examined through the eyes of managers, bargaining unit employees, and union leaders. In synthesizing the literature, therefore, I attempt to distinguish potential benefits and costs as they may be realized by these three parties to cooperative activities. Because most of these potential benefits and costs are fairly self-explanatory, I avoid any lengthy discussion but provide interested readers with citations of reports in which richer descriptions and analyses can be found. The potential benefits and costs, as the reader will surely recognize, are sometimes extrinsic or pecuniary and sometimes intrinsic or nonpecuniary, some depict more tangible outcomes than others, and some outcomes are potential benefits to one or more parties but are potential costs to another.

Potential Benefits and Costs to Management

Potential Benefits: The potential benefits to management from plant-level cooperation reflect various dimensions of the labor costs and nonlabor cost components of production. Labor costs are potentially reduced by making the production process more efficient, increasing output per unit of labor, and reducing the cost of labor per unit of product produced. Increased product demand can be derived by improving product quality, giving greater attention to customer satisfaction, and dealing more effectively with customers. By searching out ways of eliminating unnecessary overhead expenditures, minimizing waste and rework, reducing materials costs and materials handling and inventory costs, enhancing the utilization of capital equipment, and dealing more effectively with suppliers, nonlabor costs are potentially reduced. Also by minimizing unnecessary labor-management conflicts and problems and by resolving these more quickly and satisfactorily, associated lost productive time and inefficiencies are minimized. Last, cooperative efforts can potentially increase worker commitment to and identity with company goals, which lead to more aggressive efforts by employees and union leaders at being competitive and at improving workplace practices.

Drawing on the literature, the following potential benefits have been identified from a wide range and mix of cooperative efforts.

1. Increased Productivity and Efficiency

   See Voos (1987); Schuster (1984, ch.6); Cohen-Rosenthal and Burton (1987, pp. 32-33); Rosenberg and Rosenstein (1980); Contino (1986); Boyle (1986); Douty (1975); Pearlstein (1988).

2. Improved Quality of Product and Service

   See Camens (1986); Voos (1987); Boyle (1986); Katz, Kochan, and Gobeille (1983); Katz, Kochan, and Weber (1985); Smith (1986a).

3. Improved Customer Relations and Service

   See McIntosh (1988).

4. Reduced Waste and Rework

   See Boylston (1986); Katz, Kochan, and Gobeille (1983); Camens (1986).

5. Reduced Overhead, Materials Costs, and Material Handling Costs

   See Dulworth (1985); Lazes and Costanza (1984).

6. Enhanced Supplier Service

   See Roadley (1988); Cutcher-Gershenfeld (1988).

7. Improved Communications

See Driscoll (1980); Boyle (1986); Siegel and Weinberg (1982); U.S. Department of Labor (1982 and 1983); Smith (1988).

8. Improved Relationships Between Supervisors and Employees

See Fuller (1981); Boyle (1986); Burck (1981,a); Kochan, Katz and Mower (1984, pp. 134-138).

9. Reduced Grievances and Disciplinary Action

See Guest (1979); Watts (1982); U.S. Department of Labor (1982); Smith (1988b).

10. Stronger Identity and Commitment to Company Goals

See Boyle (1986); Goodman (1980); U.S. Department of Labor (1982); Walton (1985); Verma and McKersie (1987); Schuster (1989).

11. Reduced Absenteeism, Tardiness, and Turnover

See Guest (1979); Goodman (1980); Cammann, Lawler, Ledford, and Seashore (1984, p. 110); Goodman and Lawler (1979); Siegel and Weinberg (1982).

12. Increased Organizational Flexibility and Adaptability

See Cohen-Rosenthal and Burton (1987, p. 31); U.S. Department of Labor (1982 and 1983); Lawler and Drexler (1978).

Potential Costs: Organizational shifts from traditional and generally adversarial collective bargaining relationships and autocratic managerial practices (which left little room for employee or union leader participation in management decisions), demand substantial change in an organization's culture, values, and shared ideologies. These organizational shifts sometimes require sizable resources for reorientation and training of managers, supervisors, rank-and-file, and union representatives. The costs of change are not only financial but include nonpecuniary costs to many managers and supervisors in the form of perceived loss of authority, power, and status. Because of improvements in productivity and efficiency, furthermore, the perceived threat of job loss (attributable to shifting authority to employees) among managers and supervisors is heightened. In response to these potential costs, managers and supervisors are less inclined than otherwise to genuinely embrace cooperation, which necessarily reduces some of the potential company benefits identified above. There is also testimony that committee and team-based meetings are often marked by wasted or generally unproductive time, limiting management's ability to react quickly or complete production schedules in a timely fashion. In addition, when important disputes arise, the parties sometimes make unwise compromises in the name of bolstering cooperation. In summary, the literature has addressed the following potential costs of cooperation to management.

1. Added Costs for Reorientation and Training of Managers, Employees, and Union Representatives

   See Jick, McKersie, and Greenblaugh (1982); Lawler and Drexler (1978); Siegel and Weinberg (1982); U.S. Department of Labor (1982); Lee (1987).

2. Perceived Loss of Authority and Status

   See Lawler and Drexler (1978); Guest (1979); Schlesinger and Walton (1977); Rosow (1979); Jacoby (1983); Siegel and Weinberg (1982); Rosow (1986).

3. Displacement or Loss of Employment for Middle-Managers and Supervisors

   See Schlesinger and Walton (1977); Simmons and Mares (1985, ch. 13).

4. Wasted Time Spent in Meetings

   See Cutcher-Gershenfeld (1988).

Potential Benefits and Costs to Employees
Potential Benefits: Unless joint activities yield financial rewards (e.g., in the form of gainsharing) and greater employment security, the potential benefits to bargaining unit employees are largely intrinsic, as derived from more harmonious working relations and higher quality of work-

lives. The literature highlights how employees derive these potential benefits by experiencing greater participation or involvement in their work, having more say in how work gets accomplished, and improving work conditions and environments. Assuming employees prefer more harmonious over less harmonious working relations, employees potentially benefit from fewer grievance disputes and quicker problem resolution. Last, cooperative relationships often provide employees enhanced dignity, self-esteem, and pride in their work. In summary, the literature identifies and addresses the following potential benefits to employees:

1. Increased Intrinsic Rewards from the Participation or Involvement Process

   See Guest (1979); Goodman (1980); Work in America Institute, Inc. (1982, ch. 3); Parker (1985, ch. 2).

2. Greater Say in How Work Gets Accomplished

   See Kochan, Katz and Mower (1984, ch. 4).

3. Improved Working Conditions

   See U.S. Department of Labor (1983); Ruttenberg (1988).

4. Enhanced Financial Rewards From Gainsharing and Other Incentive Arrangements

   See Schuster (1989, 1984, ch. 6); Cummings and Molloy (1977, ch. 21,22); Dulworth (1985); Pearlstein (1988); Ross and Ross (1986).

5. Improved Supervisor-Employee Relationships

   See Burck (1981,a); Fuller (1981); Boyle (1986); Kochan, Katz, and Mower (1984, pp. 134-138).

6. Reduced Grievances and Quicker Resolution of Problems

   See Burck (1981a); Kochan, Katz, and Mower (1984, pp. 134-138); Smith (1988b).

7. Heightened Dignity, Self-Esteem, and Pride in Work

See U.S. Department of Labor (1983); Work in America Institute, Inc. (1982, ch. 3); McIntosh (1988).

Potential Costs: In some cases management may be perceived as promoting cooperative activities as a guise for having employees simply work harder as opposed to working smarter, which leads to greater fatigue and stress. By helping invent ways to increase productivity and efficiency, some employees fear displacement or loss of employment for themselves or co-workers. Some employees, furthermore, apparently fear having to relinquish their secret work practices, which would eliminate personal advantages in completing tasks more efficiently than others or in receiving pay incentives. More skilled or senior employees dislike sharing unwanted tasks, which is frequently required by team efforts. There is, finally, anecdotal evidence that some employees shun unwanted peer pressure to be more or less involved in cooperative activities. In summary, the literature identifies the following potential costs of cooperation to employees:

1. Working Harder, Not Necessarily Smarter

   See Oswald (1986); Simmons and Mares (1985, ch. 14).

2. Displacement or Loss of Employment From Increased Productivity and Efficiency

   See Zager (1977); Schuster (1984, ch. 6); Simmons and Mares (1985, ch. 14); Work in America Institute, Inc. (1982, ch. 3) Camens (1986); Banks and Metzgar (1989).

3. Unwanted Peer Pressure to be Involved or Not Involved

   See Spector (1986).

Potential Benefits and Costs to Unions

In weighing the potential benefits and costs of joint programs, union leaders estimate the value of joint programs in satisfying the needs and promoting the interests of (a) their members, (b) the union as an institution, and (c) themselves as leaders. The potential benefits and costs to employees described above, therefore, are weighed by union leaders. The potential benefits and costs outlined below, on the other hand, are pertinent to the union as a viable institution and to the leaders who, it can be assumed, prefer to benefit rather than be hurt politically by engaging in and supporting joint activities.

Potential Benefits: By satisfying member interests that would not otherwise be possible to satisfy except through cooperation, union leaders potentially receive recognition from members. The key here is, of course, that members reap benefits from cooperation and that they recognize these benefits were gotten via union leader involvement in establishing or modifying cooperative activities and could not have been gotten via traditional collective bargaining. This recognition, however, is sometimes thwarted by managers failing to share recognition with union leaders for benefits obtained. Cooperation also potentially provides union leaders with greater knowledge of and input into management decisionmaking, which, in turn, allows the union leadership to make better informed decisions affecting the membership and the union as an institution. Cooperation, that is, potentially gives union leaders greater access to pertinent company information, earlier notification of pending organizational changes, and opportunities to persuade management to modify their decisions.

Cooperation, in addition, potentially leads to improved communication, which (everything else the same) can lead to more harmonious interpersonal relations and trust between managers and union leaders. As an outgrowth of reduced grievances and disciplinary action, cooperation reduces the conflicts and costs associated with day-to-day contract administration. Finally, some unions have found that the organizational structures surrounding joint committee and team-based activities provide avenues for more regular input by members in union activities and policymaking. In summary, the literature identifies the following potential benefits to union leaders:

1. Recognition from Members for Improvements

    See Burck (1981,a and 1981,b); Cammann, Lawler, Ledford, and Seashore (1984, pp. 11, 21-22); Greenberg and Glaser (1980); Dyer, Lipsky, and Kochan (1977).

2. Greater Participation and Input in Management Decisions

See Fraser (1986); Cohen-Rosenthal and Burton (1987, p.20); Simmons and Mares (1985, ch. 14); Work in America Institute, Inc. (1982, ch. 4).

3. Improved Communications Between Union Leaders and Managers

See Driscoll (1980); Smith (1988b).

4. Reduced Day-to-Day Contract Administration Problems

See Cohen-Rosenthal and Burton (1987, pp. 16-17); Kochan, Katz, and Mower (1984, pp. 134-146); Watts (1982).

5. Greater Membership Input into Regular Union Activities and Policies

See Burck (1981a); Kochan, Katz, and Mower (1984, pp. 138-146); Bieber (1984, p. 34).

Potential Costs: The adjustment from traditional adversarial roles to roles that embrace cooperation is just as trying and difficult (if not more so) for union leaders as it is for managers. One potential cost to union leaders is being coopted or being perceived as coopted by management—doing management's bidding, that is, instead of protecting the interests of the union as an institution or its members more directly. It has also been reported that employers potentially use cooperative programs to undermine or bypass the union or its leadership in various ways: by appealing directly to employees for employer-initiated changes, using team-based efforts to alter collective bargaining agreements (e.g., with respect to scheduling, assignments, bidding, and job classifications); by usurping grievance procedures and union authority in resolving grievances; and by weakening the union at the bargaining table (either by creating or uncovering divisions in bargaining unit preferences over negotiable issues).

The choice to embrace cooperation and choices about the form and extent of joint activities are fraught with political conflict over proper leadership roles. Here, dissension among leaders and the rank-and-file leads to increased uncertainty of reelection. Evidence also suggests that there can be a loss of member loyalty or commitment to the union (and, hence, loss of union influence) as employees begin to accept and identify more closely with company goals. In summary, the literature identifies the following potential costs:

1. Perceived Cooptation by Management

   See Goodman (1980, p. 490); Cohen-Rosenthal and Burton (1987, pp. 17-18); U.S. Department of Labor (1982, 1983); Work in America Institute, Inc. (1982, ch. 4); Hoyer and Huszczo (1988); Strauss (1980).

2. Undermining Traditional Roles of Unions and Collective Bargaining

   See IAM Research Report (1984, pp. 16-21); UBC Bulletin (1984, pp. 41-42).

3. Heightened Political Conflict Over Leadership Role

   See Hammer and Stern (1986); Strauss (1980); Levine and Strauss (1989).

4. Increased Uncertainty of Reelection

   See Hoyer and Huszczo (1988).

5. Loss of Member Commitment and Union Influence

   See Schlesinger and Walton (1977); Kochan, Katz, and Mower (1984, pp. 134-146); Guest (1979); Watts (1982).

Fundamental Problems Encountered

When the parties experience too much of the potential cost or too little of the potential benefits outlined above, problems arise. Indeed, one could identify a multitude of day-to-day problems and frequent crises encountered in cooperative activities. Most of these problems, it appears, boil down to several more fundamental problems. First, the literature and testimony repeatedly suggest that cooperative efforts between unions and employers are based on fairly uneasy or delicate partnerships and that sufficient trust between managers and union leaders must be developed over time. When sufficient trust cannot be developed, joint activities are limited. When trust wanes or is violated, joint activities likewise wane. (Schuster 1984; Rosow 1986; Kochan, Katz, and Mower 1984.)

Sufficient commitment by all parties to cooperative efforts is also an essential ingredient to any long-run success. (See Schuster 1984, pp. 199-200; Cutcher-Gershenfield 1988; Wintergreen 1986; Kochan, Katz, and Mower 1984.) The stronger the commitment, the more intensified and diffused these cooperative activities are likely to become. Furthermore, trust and commitment appear to be inextricably intertwined. Without sufficient trust, commitment is hard to attain; and without sufficient commitment, high levels of trust are unobtainable.

In their survey of approximately 140 union representatives, Kochan, Katz, and Mower (1984) ask the extent to which "loss of union support" and "loss of plant management support" limit the expansion of the participation process. They report (see their table 5-3, p. 147) that 43 percent of the respondents do not perceive loss of plant management support as a problem. About 37 percent perceive it to be somewhat of a problem and 20 percent perceive it to be "quite a bit" or "a very great deal" of a problem. With respect to loss of union support, roughly 55 percent of the respondents report that it is not a problem, 37 percent report it to be somewhat of a problem, and about 20 percent report it to be a much more serious problem.

A third fundamental problem that arises is disenchantment and demoralization when anticipated or hoped-for gains are not gotten. When the kinds of potential benefits described above are not realized, enthusiasm for joint activities is known to wane (Camens 1986; Cutcher-Gershenfield 1988; Kochan, Katz, and Mower 1984). Kochan, Katz, and Mower report that, based on their survey of union representatives, over 60 percent of union respondents perceive "worker disenchantment" as somewhat of a problem, and nearly 35 percent perceive disenchantment as "quite a bit" or "a very great deal" of a problem. Only 4 percent respond that disenchantment among workers is not a problem. In a second related question, Kochan, Katz, and Mower report that 27 percent of the union respondents find "layoffs or other employment cutbacks" to be somewhat of a problem, whereas 53 percent find it to be a more serious problem limiting the expansion of cooperative activities.

Last, some recent literature describes how many problems arise because of the inherent difficulty of juxtaposing or balancing cooperation and more traditional collective bargaining (Bluestone 1987; Wever 1988; Hammer and Stern 1986; Smaby et al. 1988). Alternating between traditional contract negotiations and administration of contractual rights via grievance, arbitration, and discipline procedures, on one hand, and cooperative, mutually beneficial problemsolving, on the other, requires a delicate balancing of two fairly distinct processes.

Although the literature addressing these fundamental problems is rich, it remains largely testimonial and descriptive. There appear to be no scientific investigations into causes of these problems or their effects on cooperative efforts. Nearly all the literature addressing the problems of distrust, insufficient commitment, and demoralization, furthermore, has been filtered through the views of union leaders and rank-and-file; the views of managers are generally missing.

Conclusions

With very few exceptions, the existing literature about American union-management cooperation is generally descriptive and impressionistic. Although it is a rich and valuable literature, as a whole it lacks comparability across reports. It is piecemeal in its focus and, hence, lacks a broad theoretical grounding. It rarely provides any form of empirical testing of basic propositions or related specific hypotheses. The limited number of empirical investigations, furthermore, have largely attempted to determine whether or not joint efforts have had an effect on company performance and labor relations (Schuster 1983 and 1984; Katz, Kochan, and Gobeille 1983; Katz, Kochan, and Weber 1985; Katz, Kochan, and Keefe 1987; Voos 1987 and 1989). Although these empirical studies provide important evidence about outcomes (which are reviewed in chapter 4), they tell us very little about which factors or what conditions lead to more or less successful cooperative efforts. Finally, except through highly descriptive assessments, the literature also tells us little about the key factors that induce or impede the establishment of cooperative arrangements between unions and employers. In summary, our understanding of cooperation is highly fragmented and incomplete.

The purpose of this study is to help begin filling in some of these holes, first by developing more fully a general theoretical model of labor-management relations and the role of cooperation in these relations, and second by developing and testing general propositions and specific hypotheses about factors affecting decisions to cooperate and the outcomes of cooperative efforts. Cooperation between American employers and unions historically has been uncommon and short-lived; in a sharp break with history, it is widespread today. A far richer understanding of what makes cooperation work or fail is imperative, since without that understanding history will surely repeat itself, not necessarily for the right reasons.

2

A Theoretical Framework
Juxtaposing Conflict and Cooperation

The purpose of this chapter is to provide a fairly general theoretical framework of labor-management relations. By establishing some highly simplified assumptions of behavior and general propositions about the relationship between labor and management, the framework guides the analyses of decisions to embark upon, maintain, and extend cooperative activities; the salient factors affecting the outcomes of cooperation; and the key problems encountered in cooperative relationships. The framework also provides guidance in assessing several parameters of successfully moving from temporal experimentation with cooperative activities to long-term partnerships between labor and management, the subject of chapter 6.

There have been recent efforts at developing a general theoretical framework of labor-management relations by Kochan, Katz, McKersie (1986), Cooke (1985), and Barbash (1984). In all three models, environmental factors (economic, technical, and sociopolitical) play key roles in shaping the employment relationship and associated outcomes. In all three, certain organizational factors (e.g., collective bargaining structure, size, history, etc.) also shape the employment relationship and associated employment outcomes. The general environmental and organizational contexts of these models are basically extensions of Dunlop's (1958) systems framework of industrial relations.

Barbash and Cooke develop some fairly explicit assumptions of behavior of employers, employees, and union leaders. Within the environmental and organizational constraints, the parties go about maximizing or minimizing toward preferred optimal outcomes in the employment relationship. Barbash, however, is not explicit about how these behaviors within given constraints lead the parties to engage in cooperative activities. Although largely consistent with Barbash's and Cooke's models, Kochan, Katz, and McKersie fail to clearly state a full set of fundamental assumptions of behavior for all parties that would drive the employment relationship, and in turn explain employment-related outcomes. Although (unlike Barbash) Kochan, Katz, and McKersie address cooperation, except in a piecemeal fashion it is unclear how their theoretical framework predicts the decision to cooperate or explains either the intensity of those efforts or associated outcomes. In this chapter, I extend my earlier theoretical treatment of industrial relations theory (Cooke 1985) by focusing more sharply on the logic underlying cooperation vis-a-vis more traditional adversarial notions of collective bargaining.

A General Theory

Some Basic Notions

In the discussion that follows, it is held that both management and the workforce want to get "as-much-as-possible" for itself out of the employment relationship. This does not imply that each party is purely egoistic or downright greedy (although such behavior is not necessarily excluded). Nor does this imply that either party completely ignores the interests of the other party; it cannot without at some point jeopardizing its own welfare, or ultimately destroying the relationship altogether. Getting as-much-as-possible simply implies that most people prefer more over less of a desired "pie," and that this basic desire strongly governs each party's behavior.

In getting as-much-as-possible, two key dimensions of the employment relationship come into play: (1) the *overall size* or *value* of the pie available to the parties, and (2) the *division* of the pie between the parties. American history shows that, until very recently, management stakeholders were typically viewed as having sole responsibility for increasing the size or value of the pie via decisions related to operations, marketing, finance, and human resources. This view of management's exclusive domain has, historically at least, not only been widely shared by management and its stakeholders, but by the workforce and union leaders as well. Concurrently, union leaders have been viewed as agents whose primary role has been to wrest from management as-much-as-possible for the workforces they represent, leaving to management the full responsibility and task of baking a bigger pie or else giving up some of the dessert it might otherwise enjoy. Hence, until lately, management has baked the pie and fought with the union over how it was going to be divided (in Doug Fraser's words) "even before it got baked."[1]

Union-management cooperation, in contrast, reflects a concerted effort in which the workforce and its representatives share some of the responsibility and, hence, decisionmaking in baking the pie (ideally a larger pie, at a lower cost and/or of higher quality). The basic dilemma underlying cooperation is that it requires cooperation and trust. The table is laid, knives and forks clearly in sight. Each party knows where the other is coming from. When it comes to dividing the pie, however (especially when a 9-inch pie has been reduced to an 8-inch pie), the parties again pit themselves against one another. The knives are held in hand, trust diminishes if not vanishes, and there are losers and winners.

In the following subsection, I lay out a more thorough and rigorous theory than the metaphor of baking and dividing pies. Although the reader may find the exposition a bit abstract, over-simplified, and/or cumbersome for his or her tastes, the theoretical framework yields some fundamentally important propositions about cooperation, which in turn guide the empirical investigation and overall analysis.

General Assumptions and Propositions

In the abstract, one can, for the moment, imagine that there is a fixed sum of net gains derivable from a given employment relationship at any point in time. This sum of net gains is a function of both extrinsic rewards (e.g., profits and wages) and intrinsic rewards (e.g., recognition and autonomy). For ease in the discussion that follows, the combination of extrinsic and intrinsic rewards will be referred to as "utility."

This fixed sum of utility at any point in time is divided between (a) management (including all management stakeholders in the employment relationship) and (b) the workforce (including its union representatives). Assuming that both management and the workforce prefer more over less utility from the employment relationship, it follows that each party normally seeks to maximize its respective gains (hereafter called "absolute utility"). This dimension of the employment relationship is characterized by inherent conflicts of interest; what one party gets has been lost by the other or is foregone. These conflicts of interest are resolved at any point in time by relative power.

The absolute amount of utility enjoyed by either party, however, is dependent on the total utility derivable from the employment relationship. It is this variable-sum dimension of the employment relationship that inhibits either party from exercising too much power over the division of total utility. It is also this variable-sum dimension that may induce the parties to cooperate in ways that will increase total utility over time. As discussed below, the variable-sum dimension is a function of the combined organizational power of management and the workforce, not the relative power of either.

For illustration, the area within the solid-line circle in figure 2.1 depicts the total level of utility at any given point in time $(TU_{i+j,t})$. The shaded area within $TU_{i+j,t}$ envelops the absolute amount of utility derived by management $(AU_{i,t})$ in a hypothetical employment relationship, while the nonshaded area represents the absolute level of utility derived by the workforce $(AU_{j,t})$. The relative share of utility by management equals AU_i/TU_{i+j}, and the relative share of utility by workers equals AU_j/TU_{i+j}. The area under the broken-line circle $(TU_{i+j,t+n})$ depicts potential total utility in period $t+n$. The greater the circumference of the circle, the greater the total utility.

For the sake of simplicity, an underlying assumption of the present theory is that both managers and workers seek to maximize the absolute level of utility derivable from the employment relationship. Toward the goal of gaining as-much-as possible, the parties' behavior is dependent upon relative and total power. Relative power determines the distribution of a fixed sum of utility derivable from the employment rela-

Figure 2.1
Absolute, Relative, and Total Utility

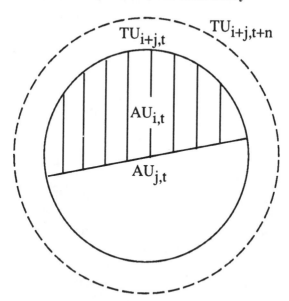

tionship. Total power, on the other hand, determines the size of the total utility available to the two parties.

Relative Power

In defining relative power, we begin with Chamberlain's definition:

> [I]f the cost to B of disagreeing on A's terms is greater than the cost of agreeing on A's terms, while the cost to A of disagreeing on B's terms is less than the cost of agreeing on B's terms, then A's bargaining power is greater than that of B's. (Chamberlain 1951, p. 221)

Chamberlain's definition requires that we estimate the perceived costs of agreeing and disagreeing in order to determine which party has greater relative power. Our interest, however, is one of identifying factors that increase or decrease the costs of agreeing and disagreeing for each party. Toward this understanding, the following implicit model of relative power is stated and briefly explained below:

$$\text{Relative Power}_i = f \left(\frac{1}{\text{cost of demands}_j} + \frac{\text{sources of power}_i}{\text{sources of power}_j} \right.$$

$$\left. + \frac{\text{bargaining skills}_i}{\text{bargaining skills}_j} \right)$$

Cost of Demands

The first component of the relative power function envelops Chamberlain's notion of the "cost of agreeing," which maintains that the relative power of party i decreases as the cost of demands upon party j increase. For example (everything else the same), a union demanding a $0.25 increase in compensation per hour is less likely to obtain that demand than if it demanded only $0.05. In the first instance, the employer will resist more because the added labor costs will have more of an effect on current profits or on product price and, hence, future profits. In addition, where profitability changes over time or differs across employers, and/or the ability to pass along costs to consumers changes over time or across employers, the cost of a $0.25 increase in hourly compensation varies; consequently, the ability of unions to obtain such increases changes over time and varies across employers. Additionally, the cost to employers and union representatives appears to vary according to perceived nonpecuniary costs associated with demands upon either party. Demands by management to involve workers in quality circles, for instance, will be perceived by various union representatives as more or less costly to their constituents' well-being or to the union as an institution. Similarly, demands by union leaders to have input into strategic decisions over plant closures will be perceived by various managers as a more or less costly intrusion on their authority or status.

In summary, the central point here is that either party has greater relative power to obtain smaller demands than larger ones (everything else constant). Hence, in comparing shifts in relative power between the parties, either over time or across organizations, by definition alone one must control for the actual or perceived costs of any demands.

Sources of Power

The second component of the relative function holds that as the sources of power available to party i to force its demands on party j increase (relative to the sources of power available to j to reject the demands of i), the relative power of i increases. With respect to Chamberlain's thesis, sources of power depict the ability of either party to impose costs of disagreeing upon the other party.

The sources of power available to the parties are derived from the economic, sociopolitical, and technical environments of the employer and from organizational features of the employer and union. The *economic* environment reflects at any given point in time the supply and demand conditions of the employer's product and labor markets. An increase in area unemployment, for instance, may increase the supply of workers to an employer. In turn, the employer's relative power at the bargaining table increases, allowing the employer to "toe the line" on demands for increased wages and benefits—if not obtain give-backs from the union. The *sociopolitical* environment affects relative power as public sentiment, laws, regulatory policies and procedures, and court decisions favor the bargaining stance of either party. The shift in the stance of the NLRB from Milwaukee Spring I to Milwaukee Spring II, for example, increased the relative power of companies to relocate production (or obtain concessions) during the life of an agreement (unless explicitly otherwise written in the contract).[2] The *technical* environment imposes constraints on either party as the substitutability of capital for labor, the continuous nature of production, and/or the strategic positioning of work groups changes or differs across organizations. The increased capabilities and reduced price tags on industrial robots over the last 15 years, for example, have effectively reduced the relative power of workforces in many industries.

Finally, certain *features of organizations* enhance the relative power of either party and/or certain groups within organizations. Of particular importance are the organizational structures, philosophies, and resources of employers and unions. Compare, if you will, two companies, identical with the exception that Company A has all of its ten manufacturing plants organized by the same national union, and Company B has only two of its ten plants organized by the same national union. Given Company B's ability to shift production from its two unionized plants to its eight nonunion plants in the event of a strike, the union's relative power is greater in Company A than in Company B.

Bargaining Skill

Relative bargaining skill is the third component of the relative power function. In attempting to maximize the relative share of total utility, each party attempts to change the perceptions of the other regarding the sources of power available to each and the costs of demands on the other. Given the complexity and subjective nature inherent in the assessment of the sources of power and the pecuniary/nonpecuniary costs of demands, one can imagine that there is significant opportunity for changing perceptions (and hence demands). That party which is more skilled or adept at changing the perceptions of its opponent (of course to the given party's benefit) effectively increases the given party's relative power over the other.

In the context of union-management relations, these bargaining skills are especially important during regular contract negotiations, as the terms and conditions of employment are established or modified. Relative bargaining skills, however, also come into play during the life of agreements. No written agreement—in spite of its length, detail, and duration—can possibly determine all the terms and conditions of employment. Hence the parties must, in effect, continue negotiating over formal and informal rules governing the employment relationship. In its most obvious form, disputes over the agreements are resolved through grievance and discipline procedures, including arbitration. Here, relative negotiation skills play a significant role in determining how total utility is divided. That party which is more skilled, for instance, at interpreting or utilizing to their advantage (1) the rights and responsibilities arising from the contract and past practices, and (2) the facts surrounding disagreements, effectively increases the given party's relative power (Meyer and Cooke 1988).

In addition to these day-to-day negotiations over the interpretation and application of contracts, unions may also attempt to influence management decisions at a more strategic level, such as management decisions regarding expansion or shrinkage of operations or capital investments. The birth of GM's Saturn Corporation jointly devised by UAW and GM representatives is perhaps the outstanding example along these lines.[3] Again, relative negotiation skills can make a difference.

Total Power

Total utility derivable from the employment relationship is determined by the combination of human and technical capacity of the employing organization, constrained by the economic and sociopolitical environments of the organization. In attempting to maximize total utility, the parties rely on total organizational power, which is the ability of an organization to extract from its environment the kind and magnitude of benefits preferred.

The total organization power function can be stated as:

$$\text{Total Organizational Power} = f \left(\frac{\text{Human} + \text{Technical Capacity of Organization}}{\text{Economic} + \text{Sociopolitical Environmental Constraints}} \right)$$

The capacity of an organization to produce a product or provide a service at a profit is a function of both human capacity and technical capacity. *Human capacity* is the combined capacity of all stakeholders of the organization, from the top strategic decisionmaking offices down to the shop floor. Those organizations (1) employing the most talented and productive individuals across and throughout all the managerial and employee ranks, and (2) whose managerial processes and practices and structure maximize the combined productive utilization of all individuals, in turn maximize human capacity.

Technical capacity represents the combination of all the types of technologies utilized throughout the organization, how these technologies are integrated, and how well these technologies and their integration are utilized in production or in the provision of services by all members of the organization. Across organizations and over time, the availability of less costly and/or more productive technologies and innovations differ, as well as the ability of the organization to integrate and utilize the technologies in the most productive and efficient manner.

In addition to the human and technical capacity of an organization, total organizational power is determined by the constraints (or lack thereof) imposed by the economic and sociopolitical environments. With respect to constraints of the *economic environment*, by way of example, the reader hardly needs to be reminded of the changing economics of global competition. Off-shore competition continues to penetrate both the domestic and foreign markets of many American businesses. As demand for American-made products falls, profits shrink, employees are laid off, concessions may be negotiated, assets stripped, and facilities closed. In short, total utility for many companies diminishes. In response to the impact of heightened global competition, organizational capacity adjusts: organizations restructure through merger, acquisition, or joint ventures; centralize or decentralize operations; they replace top executives; they make bold capital investments in new and old facilities both here and off-shore; they transfer production off-shore; or they restate corporate visions with new concentration, for example, on product quality improvement, employee involvement in management decisionmaking, or cooperation with unions.

Sociopolitical environments also differ across organizations and over time, sometimes imposing greater and sometimes imposing lesser constraints on organizational capacity. Several examples come quickly to mind. Recent deregulation of the trucking and airline industries has certainly affected the total organizational power of companies within these industries, resulting in widespread reorganization. Recent protective U.S. trade practices in the steel, textile, and auto industries offset diminishing total organizational power for some companies. The federal government's break-up of AT&T altered the organizational capacity of AT&T and effectively increased the total organizational power of its competitors within the telecommunications industry.

Relative Power v. Total Organizational Power

Based on perceptions of relative power and total power, workers and managers seeking to maximize the absolute level of utility must weigh the expected net gains from (a) relying solely on relative power or (b) also working jointly to increase total organizational power. Under the assumption of maximizing behavior, we must hold that each party seeks to utilize that combination of relative and total power it perceives as best serving its own interests. Hence, each party weighs the perceived costs and benefits of various combinations of relative and total power activities that could maximize its absolute utility. Both parties, however, must come or be forced to the same conclusion on the appropriate mix. Historically, with few exceptions until lately, this conclusion has been that management has sole responsibility for managing total organizational power (and, hence, total utility), and that both parties utilize their relative power to maximize their relative utility (and, hence, absolute utility).

In attempting to understand the recent widespread move toward plant-level cooperative activities (intentionally undertaken to increase total organizational power), we need to ask: what are the key factors that have changed the perceptions of one or the other party or both parties such that the perceived net benefit from cooperation has changed significantly? Later, factors that increase the perceived benefits or reduce the perceived costs of cooperation are identified. For the moment, let us stay at a more general theoretical level.

In deciding that some degree of cooperation will lead to increased utility for each party, the parties are attempting to (a) increase organizational capacity and/or (b) reduce the constraints of the economic or sociopolitical environments directly. Herein, I focus on efforts aimed at increasing organizational capacity at the corporate and plant levels. An example of cooperative efforts to reduce environmental constraints is the ongoing lobbying efforts of both manufacturers and unions in the textile and steel industries to have Congress embrace protective trade legislation.

With respect to increasing total organizational power, the following kinds of behavior are observed: (a) one party relinquishes some absolute utility (and, hence, relative utility) with the expectation that this will increase total utility in subsequent periods (for which that party regains its relinquished absolute utility but not *ipso facto* its relative utility), or (b) both parties voluntarily alter the set of work rules for which each party believes that relinquished absolute utility will subsequently be regained.

Figures 2.2 and 2.3 should help illustrate these concepts. In figure 2.2, the solid-line circle (TU_t) depicts total utility in period t. Presume for the moment that the potential total utility in subsequent periods is reflected by the broken-line circle (TU_{t+n}). To obtain the greater potential total utility in t+n, however, changes in the existing utility must come about. One option is for the parties to exchange control of selected work rules, without simultaneously altering relative utility (e.g., workers might exchange restrictive work rules for a gainsharing plan). Diagrammatically, the line of demarcation of relative utility, RU, rotates to RU′. Such trade-offs increase total utility from TU_t to TU_{t+n}, reflecting the assumed maximizing behavior, since absolute utility increases for both parties. A second option illustrated in figure 2.2 is the shift from RU to RU″. The reduction in relative utility (and, hence, absolute utility) by party j depicts a calculated move by j in period t as a means of obtaining $AU_{j,t+n}$. Party j would behave as such only if what is added in absolute utility for j in period t+n is perceived to be greater than what is to be relinquished in period t. Although relative utility in this instance becomes smaller in period t+n, party j has behaved in such a way that absolute utility is maximized over time.

Now consider figure 2.3, where expectations (e.g., about international competition) are such that total utility will be reduced in period t+1 (depicted by the –•– circle). When expectations about obtaining greater total utility in subsequent periods (e.g., returning to TU_t) are insufficient to compel the parties to behave cooperatively during period t +1, the parties will rely on relative power to wrest away more absolute

Figure 2.2
Expected Increases in Total Utility in Period t + n

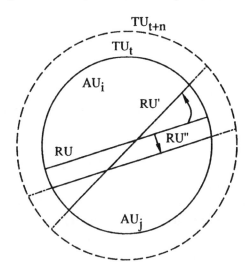

Figure 2.3
Expected Reductions in Total Utility in t + 1
and Expected Increases in Total Utility in t + n

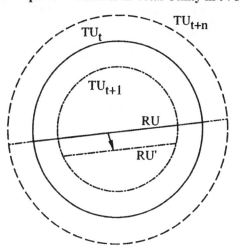

utility from one another. This has become known as "concession" or "give-back" negotiations. As illustrated, the shift in the relative power position of the parties from RU to RU' has allowed party i to lose less (if any) of its absolute utility between periods, while party j has lost some absolute utility between periods. Of course if the changes in the economic and/or sociopolitical environments that caused the reduction in total utility do not effectively alter the relative power positions of the parties, then no shift in relative utility will be generated. Consequently, both parties experience proportionately equal reductions in absolute utility.

A fundamental dilemma becomes apparent as the parties simultaneously weigh relative and total power options and requisite behavior. Given that, historically, employers and unions have largely attended to resolving conflicts of interest via the exercise of relative power, it would appear to be a safe presumption to hold that the appeal of resolving conflicts of interest supersedes the appeal of working jointly on mutual interests. A key challenge to unions and employers, therefore, is to find ways to juxtapose or balance the resolution of conflicts of interest with the pursuit of mutual interests. That balance, however, goes well beyond the efforts of the parties at the bargaining table to jointly solve problems. These "integrative bargaining" practices have long been a part of the collective bargaining experience (see Walton and McKersie 1965, chapter 5). That balance, furthermore, goes beyond joint committees established to mutually resolve problems like health and safety, training, and employee assistance. These limited joint problemsolving efforts may be viewed as an extended form of integrative bargaining and are likely precursors to the kind of joint programs to be examined herein.

Sharing Gains From Cooperation

Among those parties choosing to cooperate, it can be assumed that each party wants its fair share of any increase in total utility derivable from cooperative activities. The parties ultimately must decide upon an appropriate fair share for each, presumably based on each party's contribution to added total utility via cooperation. In deciding on a fair share, the parties must first determine the amount of total utility that has been derived from cooperative efforts—an amount that must be distinguishable from any gains in total utility not derived from cooperative efforts (e.g., gains derived from decisions about technology investments, acquisitions, product development, marketing, etc. for which the union may not have participated in making).

By way of example, assume that in period $t+n$, total utility increased by X amount, where $X=NC+C$, and where NC equals the gain from noncooperative activities and C equals the gain from cooperative activities. As diagrammed in figure 2.4, the unshaded area marked NC depicts increases in total utility that would have been obtained without cooperation. This gain is, in turn, distributed via relative power, a mechanism which is acceptable (albeit, perhaps begrudgingly) to both parties. The shaded area marked C in figure 2.4 depicts increases in total utility only obtainable through cooperation. Here the parties can be assumed to seek their fair share; shares not based on notions of relative power but on notions of contribution to C.

One can readily imagine that sharing any gains from cooperation is wrought with difficult assessments about (a) how much of any increases in total utility are attributable to noncooperative and cooperative efforts, and (b) what proportion of any increases in total utility attributable to cooperative efforts are due to each party's contribution.

These difficult assessments inevitably lead to problems, problems which diminish if not destroy cooperative relations (as discussed in detail in chapter 6), when the parties are unable to resolve them in mutually satisfactory ways. For the sake of illustration, assume that the union's contribution to added total utility via cooperative efforts is 75 percent—or at least perceived to be by the union. Assume, however, that management's relative power would be sufficient to extract 50 percent of that added total utility. If management were to impose its relative power will on the union, the union would forego 25 percent of added total utility it perceives itself to have contributed. The union, therefore, may obtain more absolute utility through cooperation than without, but management gains even more in relative terms. This relative difference raises an obvious dilemma. The process of cooperation requires ele-

Figure 2.4
Sharing Cooperative and Noncooperative
Gains to Total Utility in t + n

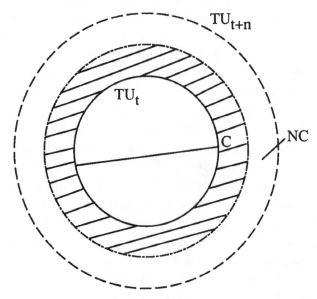

ments of sufficient trust and fairness, which are not required in adversarial relations. To divide the added utility derived from cooperation via relative power diminishes, therefore, the necessary trust and fairness underlying cooperation. In turn, the intensity of cooperative efforts is diminished (if not destroyed), which, as discussed in chapter 4, reduces the magnitude of gains from cooperative activities. Upon reducing the added total utility from cooperation, management (in our example) consequently also loses added utility. In summary, each party must weigh (a) any losses in absolute utility caused by using relative power to divide cooperative gains against (b) the absolute utility derived from cooperative gains, which are divided fairly according to what each party contributes to the added total utility from cooperation.

Feedback From Experience

Because the decisions and behavior of the parties are shaped or constrained by *subjective* interpretations of the costs of demands, the sources of power, and the net benefits of any mix of cooperation and hard bargaining, feedback from experience (both internal and external to the organization) plays a critical role in determining (and, hence, understanding) the behavior of the parties. This feedback mechanism or learning curve effect on perceptions and, in turn, presumably on behavior, applies to all the underlying dimensions of the relative power and total power functions.

Since employers and unions traditionally have had very limited experience in cooperation, the feedback mechanism is obviously quite important to the maintenance, as well as expansion of joint labor-management activities. In particular, depending upon the magnitude of any problems encountered and/or changes in the expected outcomes of joint endeavors, the parties can be expected to adjust the intensity, extensiveness, or content of joint activities in an effort to effectively increase organizational capacity and, hence, total organizational power.

The perceptions of outcomes and the relative costs of problems encountered are also likely to change with the longevity of joint programs, given the possibility of diminishing returns of these efforts over time or abrupt changes in expected outcomes (e.g., as may arise from a disheartening round of concession bargaining). These changes in perception over time can result in subsequent termination of programs. In the chapters that follow, I explore these perceptions of outcomes and, moreover, attempt to track how perceptions change over the life of programs.

Potential Benefits and Costs of Cooperation
Vis-a-Vis Relative Power Options

Both management and its stakeholders and the workforce and its selected union representatives must sort through the options underlying both the relative and total power functions. In sorting through these options the parties, in effect, weigh the perceived potential costs and benefits (both pecuniary and nonpecuniary) of a wide range of possible actions, ranging from no cooperation to extensive cooperation. Assuming that the parties act rationally in selecting among available options, the parties will behave in ways at least perceived to be most beneficial to them (i.e., that which maximizes absolute utility). This maximizing or optimizing behavior, however, is based on *subjective* expectations about various costs and benefits, is constrained by incomplete information and limited experience, and is sometimes influenced by inaccurate or misleading information. Furthermore, and very important, organizational decisionmaking is quite complex, as it involves a large cast of individuals with varying interests and varying degrees of authority and influence. This decisionmaking process differs, of course, across employers and across unions.

Bearing these caveats in mind, the decision to cooperate must satisfy two general conditions:

(1) Each party (management, the workforce, and union leadership) must perceive that the benefits from proposed joint programs outweigh the costs.

(2) Each party must perceive that the net benefit from cooperation is greater than the net benefit derived from exclusive utilization of relative power.

The basic thesis herein is that the likelihood that parties establish and are able to manage successful joint programs varies directly with the following perceptions for each party:

a. higher perceived benefits from cooperation;
b. lower perceived costs of cooperation;
c. higher perceived costs of relative power options; and
d. lower perceived benefits of relative power options.

In modeling the factors that influence the joint decision of the parties to establish and manage successful cooperative programs, therefore, we must turn to identifying factors and circumstances that are associated with either increasing or decreasing these perceived benefits and costs.

In chapter 1, potential benefits and costs and fundamental problems associated with cooperative activities were identified. There is no need to revisit that synthesis in this chapter, but several observations about the difficulty of weighing potential benefits and costs is warranted. Subsequently, perceived benefits and costs associated with exercising relative power options (e.g., concession bargaining, subcontracting, etc.) are discussed.

Assessing Potential Benefits and Costs of Cooperation

Several general observations about the above costs and benefits are warranted. First, costs and benefits can be either extrinsic or intrinsic in nature. Although each party is expected to weigh both extrinsic and intrinsic variables, it should be underscored that the parties are typically weighing apples and oranges. Management, for instance, may be able to weigh (a) the perceived reduction in production costs attributable to increased productivity, improved product quality, and reduction in scrappage against (b) the incurred education and training cost for workers and supervisors (in, say, statistical process control techniques, problemsolving, and teamwork methods). But how does management then compare those extrinsic costs and benefits to the intrinsic costs and benefits associated with, say, perceived loss of status for middle managers and supervisors, or improved communications between and among white-collar and blue-collar workers? The key point to be made here is that the literature addresses both extrinsic and intrinsic costs and benefits of cooperation, but it is silent with regard to how the parties go about weighing potential intrinsic costs and benefits. In part, this is a measurement problem. How does one measure, for example, the benefits of improved communication? In addition, this is a valuation problem. How does one place a cost-benefit value on improved communication, which can then be compared to other intrinsic costs and benefits and, moreover, to extrinsic costs and benefits?

A second observation is about the distinction between what may be called, for present purposes, primary and secondary outcome variables. Secondary outcome variables may have value in and of themselves, but they also lead to more tangible primary outcomes. An example may best illustrate this distinction. Improved communication or harmony between managers and employees (secondary outcomes) may be valued outcomes in and of themselves, but they may also lead to other outcomes such as fewer grievances, enhanced job security, or increased productivity (primary outcomes). The literature on joint programs is again silent on how the perceived costs and benefits of primary outcomes are weighed or stack up against secondary outcomes. In most cases, one can imagine that primary outcomes get closer to the "bottom-line" thinking of the parties and, hence, play a more important role in the decision to embark upon and/or maintain joint programs. We have much to uncover, however, with respect to what outcomes are primary or secondary in nature; how this distinction may differ between management, workers, and union leaders; and how much weight is given to each type of outcome as the parties go about deciding the fate of cooperation.

The third observation is that some potential outcome variables reflect costs or benefits specific to a given party (e.g., increased employee commitment to the union primarily benefits the union leadership). Other outcome variables reflect costs or benefits to more than one party (e.g., a reduced grievance load saves both management and the union leadership lost time and resources in resolving grievances). Going one step further, what may be viewed as a benefit to one party can alternatively be perceived as a cost to another party. For instance, more rank-and-file autonomy may be viewed as a benefit by a work unit but not by its supervisor.

Finally, the potential magnitude of any cost or benefit is bound to differ across organizations as circumstances differ. Take, for illustration, an organization with a very low grievance rate. It has less to gain from reducing grievances through joint program activities than an organization with a very high grievance rate.

In summary, the salient variables identified in the existing literature that appear to be weighed by the parties (a) include both extrinsic and intrinsic costs and benefits, which makes meaningful comparisons very difficult; (b) represent what may be called primary and secondary outcomes, which may differ across parties and, again, make comparisons very difficult; and (c) may reflect costs and benefits specific to one party or shared by other parties, or may reflect costs to one party but benefits to another. Finally, the reader should bear in mind that the potential magnitude of any cost or benefit is bound to differ across employers, workforces, and union leadership.

Assessing Potential Benefits and Costs of Exercising Relative Power Options

Toward maximizing their own absolute utility without cooperation, employers attempt to bolster their relative power, and, when possible, increase total utility. Within our theoretical framework, these efforts are concentrated in altering organizational features (via the relative power function) and altering the human and technical capacity of the firm (via the total organizational power function). From the vantage point of unions, pursuit of increases or maintenance of their own absolute utility (without cooperation), rests solely with reshaping organizational features (via the relative power function).

From a more practical plane of analysis, we need to examine the salient relative power options. Both the popular and more academic literature identify several key management options: concession bargaining, subcontracting, curtailing operations and closing plants, substituting computer-based automation for labor, and deunionizing. Except for improving organizing activities, union options reflect, for the most part, defensive strategies to the above management options.

Other than in the broadest of terms, the literature has little to say about the estimated costs and benefits of the various relative power options. Assuming, however, that top management is driven to maximize profits for the company as a whole and that middle and lower management in production have been directed to maximize efficiency, quality, and productivity and minimize labor costs, it follows that management decisions are viewed by managers as providing the greatest net benefit to the company. It is evident that, except for concession bargaining, no option selected is based strictly on reducing labor costs, albeit the reduction of labor costs may be an important if not a primary factor in selecting options.

In examining the perceived costs and benefits of relative power options, several dimensions of the subject are worth underscoring. First, most key options appear to be more aggressively pursued under increasingly competitive, if not adverse, economic circumstances. In theoretical terms, total organizational utility has diminished or is expected to diminish, short of some organizational adjustments. Second, although management may be able to estimate the direct net benefit from a selected option (e.g., the projected net savings in materials handling, inventory, labor costs, etc., from subcontracting), the indirect potential costs of lower employee morale, union-management hostility, and heightened insecurity are not readily ascertainable. One might even surmise that in an already existing adversarial union-management relationship, indirect costs associated with relative power options may have been given little if any consideration. Still, these are costs, which later may become apparent in higher grievance rates, absenteeism and tardiness, and in reduced productivity or product quality. Finally, any net gains or losses from any option differ across employers and unions, and are determined in part by certain controlling or intervening variables (e.g., market conditions).

Mixing Conflict and Cooperation
A Summary

Joint labor-management programs designed to improve company performance and the labor-management relationship have recently become widespread in manufacturing because the companies, unions, and employees involved have come to perceive (at least for the moment) that the net gains from cooperative efforts to each party outweigh the net gains from exclusive reliance on traditional uses of relative and total power. The theory presented in this chapter, as well as American history, suggests that when the relative power of a party increases sufficiently at any point in time, that party will exercise its added relative power to increase its own absolute utility and at the perceived expense of the other party. It follows, therefore, that in many cases where the parties cooperate, one party (as a practical matter, almost always the employer) will first pursue the kind of relative power options described above. After the net benefits from these options have been reaped and expected net benefits from further usage of relative power options have been significantly reduced, both parties may come to a similar conclusion: greater net benefit can be derived from joint efforts than from the continued exclusive exercise of relative power options. It is at that point where the parties begin to design and implement joint programs.

In other cases, the reduction in total utility experienced as the pie shrinks may not significantly alter the relative power of the parties. In these cases the loss of utility by both parties may trigger an examination of the potential costs and benefits of cooperation, as it becomes apparent that the net gain from attempting to use the relative power options is zero, if not negative. Once both parties perceive that the potential net benefits of cooperation outweigh the potential costs, then the parties begin to design and implement joint programs.

None of the above suggests, however, that companies and unions have not exercised their relative power in conjunction with joint program activities. In those cases where they do, the parties must find a means of satisfactory balance that allows for the coexistence of the two processes. Shifts in relative power are bound to occur over time, and the gaining party invariably will be inclined to exercise that added relative power. Consequently, when the perceived net benefits of relative power options begin to outweigh the perceived net benefit of cooperation, the parties must be prepared for the potential exercise of relative power and its implications for the continuance of joint program activities. Because the relative power options heighten conflict, the use of these options threaten, if not ultimately undermine, the cooperative process.

NOTES

1.   Quote selected from presentation made by Mr. Douglas Fraser (former President of the UAW) at the University of Michigan, February 1, 1987.

2.   See the case of Milwaukee Spring Division of Illinois Coil Spring Company v. UAW Local 547, NLRB Decisions and Orders, 265 NLRB 28 (1982) and Second Court of Appeals decision, 765 F.2d 175 (1985).

3.   See James Treece, "Here Comes Saturn," Business Week, April 9, 1990, pp. 56-62.

3

Choosing to Cooperate

Company Strategies and Plant Programs

The central objectives of this chapter are to examine companywide strategic choices to pursue union-management cooperation and to describe joint activities at the plant level in companies that have chosen to cooperate. To set the stage for these investigations, however, I first briefly describe the economic context in which important shifts in companywide strategies have occurred, and second I review the limited literature about these companywide strategic choices. Because the empirical evidence used to examine company strategies and plant-level joint activities are based on several survey data collections, these data collections are then reviewed. Subsequently, I examine companywide strategic choices with respect to factors influencing these choices and the implementation of these strategies over the 1975 to 1986 period. Finally, I describe in some detail plant-level joint activities.

Market Factors Inducing Change

During the latter half of the 1970s and throughout much of the 1980s, the economic environment was marked by uncharacteristic short-term volatility, coupled with the emergence of long-run global and domestic nonunion competitive threats and other long-run trends demanding change in traditional collective bargaining relationships.

Short-Run Forces

With respect to short-run forces, several factors are illustrative of substantial market volatility or instability. First, annual nationwide unemployment rates bounced erratically from 5 percent in 1973 to a postwar high of 9.4 percent in 1983.[1] In some regions of the U.S., unemployment rose to much higher levels. During the same period, annual inflation rates likewise jumped and dropped as much as 12 percentage points, with both the Consumer Price Index and Producer Price Index reaching nearly 14 percent in 1980.[2] Between 1977 and 1981, the annual average prime rate charged by banks for short-term business loans rose from 7 percent to a post-War high of nearly 19 percent.[3] The annual inflation-adjusted U.S. exchange rate rose sharply from a low of 84 points in 1978 to 130 points by 1985 (1973 indexed at 100 points). These real exchange rates then dropped nearly as sharply to 88 points in 1988.[4] Finally, crude oil (and to a lesser extent natural gas) prices rose and fell rapidly over the 1973 through 1988 period. Indeed, crude oil prices jumped nearly fivefold from $1.25 per million Btu in 1973 to nearly $6 per million Btu in 1981 (in constant 1982 dollars).[5]

By 1988, unemployment, inflation, prime interest rates, real exchange rates, and energy costs returned to their pre-1975 levels. One might be inclined to conclude, therefore, that these market factors have taken their short-run toll on American businesses and unions and that we have returned to normalcy or stability in the market place. The volatility of this recent period, however, vividly demonstrates that were the future to hold similar periods of volatility, companies and unions that have not become more flexible and adaptable in their relations will find themselves at a competitive disadvantage. And that disadvantage could, indeed, be substantial.

Long-Run Forces

In addition to short-run volatility, several long-run forces are at work. First, the proportion of all employees represented by unions in the U.S. has dropped steadily since the mid-1950s, from roughly 35 percent to under 17 percent today. In the private sector, the proportion has dropped to 13 percent.[6] Although the accuracy of any given union penetration estimates can be questioned, the precipitous decline in union penetration cannot. The threat of rising domestic nonunion competition has rather obvious implications for unionized companies and for unionized facilities within multiplant companies partially unionized.

In addition to steadily rising domestic nonunion competition, global competition likewise clearly poses a long-run threat to much of American industry. The import penetration ratio (value of imports over total value of domestic shipments and imports) for all manufacturing rose from 7 percent in 1974 to 13 percent in 1986.[7] For some industries, the rise in import penetration has been far more dramatic. The value of durable good imports alone rose dramatically from $150 billion in 1983 to $300 billion in 1989 (in constant 1982 dollars). Although U.S. exports likewise rose dramatically after 1983, total goods and services imports have continued to outrun exports; a difference that reached as high as $130 billion in 1986 but narrowed to $56 billion in 1989.[8]

Major investments in computer-aided technology may also be viewed as a long-run force at work. North American investments in robotics rose more than fourfold (in constant dollars) between 1981 and 1985 to $525 million—tapering off, however, to $430 million in 1988. After dropping sharply from roughly $2.4 to $1.6 billion between 1982 and 1983, capital expenditures in computer-aided machine tools rebounded by 1985 and rose to $2.8 billion in 1988.[9]

A fourth long-run force at work is the steadily rising cost of medical care and associated benefits. Indexed to 1982 costs, the real cost of medical care has risen threefold since 1975; and there is no indication that these costs will soon be contained.[10]

Although a number of other important long-run forces at work can be identified (for example, effects of deregulation of the transportation industry, divestiture of AT&T, the aging population, and rising female labor force participation and divorce rates), the four long-run forces described sufficiently document the need for restructuring labor-management relationships. Although the form of any restructuring is debatable, those unionized companies that cannot adapt to these long-run forces are very likely to become uncompetitive.

Companywide Labor Relations Strategies: The Literature

The forces at work described above have inevitably required adjustment by unionized companies, either to maintain or regain competitive advantages or in some cases to minimize further erosion of competitive advantages. Recent case studies undertaken by researchers associated with the Sloan School of Management at M.I.T. identify three sufficiently distinct and emerging corporate labor-relations strategies: one in which the purpose is to avoid if not reduce union representation (call it Union-Avoidance), another in which the parties choose to cooperate (call it Cooperation), and a third encompassing both union-avoidance and cooperative activities (call it Mixed).[11]

The *Union-Avoidance* strategy is basically a highly adversarial strategy that encompasses several kinds of activities designed to reduce the proportion of plants unionized. Toward this end, Union-Avoiders aggressively campaign against the unionization of existing, newly opened, or acquired nonunion facilities. Although it comes as no surprise that employers generally prefer to operate in a nonunion environment, recent evidence reported by Freedman (1979, 1985) indicates that top management of large firms places a high priority on avoiding unionization of the firm's nonunion facilities. According to the Freedman surveys, 31 percent of large, double-breasted firms (i.e., those firms with union and nonunion establishments) in 1977 and 45 percent in 1983 reported that it was more important to them to keep as much of the company nonunion than it was to achieve the most favorable bargain possible.

In addition, Union-Avoiders make greater capital investments in nonunion than in unionized plants, reduce employment in unionized plants while increasing employment in nonunion plants, and, where possible, seek decertification of unions. Tough positional negotiations that demand concessionary bargains over wages, benefits, and work rules are standard practice. Joint union-management activities at the plant level are anomalies; they are sometimes used as temporary playgrounds for experimentation with employee involvement, with the lessons learned to be transferred to nonunion plants. In many, if not most cases, the Union-Avoidance strategy is an attack on the very legitimacy of union representation.

The *Cooperation* strategy is an endorsement of joint decisionmaking at the plant level. Generally, union participation is formalized through the establishment of committee-based and/or team-based programs. The purpose of these joint programs is to improve company performance via increased efficiency and productivity, higher product quality, and better supplier/customer services. In some settings, union leaders participate in strategic business decisions. Although Cooperators do not engage in aggressive union-avoidance or deunionization activities, they do not relinquish relative power advantages.

Companies pursuing a *Mixed* strategy are double-breasted companies that engage in many of the above union-avoidance activities in their nonunion operations but engage in cooperative efforts in their unionized operations. These companies, in short, are pursuing strategies that embrace simultaneously what might appear to be two irreconcilable approaches to union-management relations.

In addition to the case reports about the above strategies, in their analysis of the 1983 Conference Board survey of large companies, Kochan, McKersie, and Chalykoff (1986) briefly report on a model of the determinants of the extent of "workplace innovations" across companies (see their table 2, page 493). Although not described in detail in their report, the following factors are reported as statistically significant in their regression estimation of factors influencing the extent of workplace innovations.

- When corporate executives have emphasized a union-avoidance strategy, the extent of work place innovations in unionized facilities is lower.

- The more the union(s) participates in workplace innovations, the more extensive are these innovations.

- The greater the influence of line executives *vis-a-vis* industrial relations executives, the more extensive are workplace innovations in unionized establishments. (Presumably, line executives are not as frozen in traditional labor relations practices as are industrial relations executives.)

- Larger companies engage in more extensive workplace innovations.

Perhaps just as interesting as the statistically significant estimates, are two insignificant estimates. First, Kochan et al. do not find a statistically significant relationship between "percentage of firm organized" and extent of workplace innovations. Second, executive perceptions of "competitive pressures on the firm (foreign and domestic)" are not significantly related to extent of workplace innovations. Generally speaking, these latter results are at odds with the Cooke and Meyer (1990) results summarized below and as discussed by Kochan et al. (page 494), apparently at odds with their own expectations.

Plant Manager, Local Union Officer, and Executive Survey Data Collection

Three separate but complementary data collections were conducted for this study. The first surveyed plant-level managers, the second surveyed their local union leader counterparts, and the third surveyed executives of companies parent to the plants surveyed. These survey data are supplemented by a variety of secondary data sources.

As discussed in chapter 1, one of the limitations of the literature is the lack of comparability across single case study observations. An addition to the current literature, therefore, is the collection of comparable data across establishments. Short of having unlimited resources and unlimited access to organizations, however, we necessarily sacrifice details obtained through intensive observation and data collection at a given organization in exchange for greater comparability and generalization of less detailed observations across a wide sample of organizations. In order to obtain opinions and impressions across a wide sample of companies, plants, and local unions, each organizational response is based on a single response from plant managers, local union leaders, and company executives, respectively.

The data collection began by randomly selecting 430 unionized manufacturing companies listed in *A Directory to Collective Bargaining Agreements: Private Sector, 1982*. The directory, published by Microfilming Corporation of America in 1983, is based on collective bargaining agreements filed with the U.S. Bureau of Labor Statistics in 1982 (or agreements that were filed before but encompassed 1982). Approximately 1,800 agreements across all manufacturing are listed. Although agreements affect 900 or more employees, listed agreements are sometimes master agreements covering more than one facility. Any given facility, consequently, need not employ 900 or more bargaining unit employees.

Company names were then matched with Dun's Marketing Service's DMI unpublished files. These files provide names, addresses, phone numbers, and employment figures at the establishment level. After an extensive telephone search, only 350 of the 430 establishments could be located. The establishments that could not be located apparently had been sold or closed between 1980 and 1986. Given the extent of company mergers, acquisitions, and plant closures during the early through mid-1980s, this less than 20 percent turnover of unionized plants would not be unexpected.

Labor relations managers or plant managers identified through the initial telephone inquiries as the most knowledgeable with respect to union-management activities and plant production were surveyed. After three requests for a response, 55 percent (194) returned useable questionnaires. The data base compiled through this survey will hereafter be referred to as the "Plant Manager Survey." (See appendix A for a copy of the questionnaire.)

Through the initial telephone inquiries to plant management, the telephone number of the local union office was obtained. The local union office was then contacted to explain the purpose and scope of the survey and to identify the top local officer most familiar with the given plant. These officers were then surveyed. After three requests for responses, 33 percent (114) returned useable questionnaires. Of the 114 responses, 74 were from unions representing employees in plants for which plant manager responses were also obtained. The remaining 40 were not matchable to any plant manager response. The data base compiled through this survey will hereafter be referred to as the "Union Officer Survey." (See appendix B for a copy of the questionnaire.)

In the survey of plant managers, respondents were asked to identify the top labor relations or human resource executive at the parent company or division headquarters who would be most familiar with labor relations at all the company's plants. Initial telephone calls were made to headquarter executives to explain the purpose and scope of the survey and to check whether the executive identified from the Plant Manager Survey was the most knowledgeable executive for the purpose of completing the survey. After two follow-up requests for responses, 121 useable questionnaires were returned. Because some headquarters responding were parent to more than one plant in the sample, headquarter information is available for 135 (or 71 percent) of the 194 plants represented in the Plant Manager Survey. The data base compiled through this survey will hereafter be referred to as the "Headquarters Executive Survey." (See appendix C for a copy of the questionnaire.)

Analysis of Headquarters Executive Survey Data

In the Headquarters Executive Survey, executives were queried regarding company policy toward union representation of nonunion plants and executive attitudes toward the establishment of joint programs in their plants. With some adjustment explained below, responses to these questions are used to classify companies as pursuing one of three grand labor relations strategies.

Respondents were asked to complete the following two statements:

   (1) "In general, it is company policy to
_____ strongly oppose _____ oppose _____ remain neutral to
union representation of nonunion manufacturing plants."
   (2) "In general, company executives are
_____ not in favor of _____ in favor of _____ indifferent to
joint management-union programs or activities."

The responses to these two questions are cross tabulated below.

When respondents reported it was company policy to strongly oppose or oppose union activities, the company is categorized as following a Union-Avoidance strategy. Companies reportedly strongly opposed to

Cross-Tabulation of Responses

Executive stance toward unionization	Executive stance toward joint programs		
	Not in favor	Indifferent to	In favor
Strongly Oppose	17	10	27
Oppose	5	8	32
Neutral To	0	4	16

union representation and at the same time in favor of joint activities are categorized as following a Mixed strategy. Companies reportedly neutral to union representation of nonunion plants and in favor of joint activities are categorized as following a Cooperation strategy.

There is some question as to whether the 32 companies opposed to unionization (but not strongly opposed) and in favor of joint activities are pursuing Cooperation or Mixed strategies. Here a comparison is made using the percent of plants with formalized joint programs and the percent of plants unionized in 1986. Of the 32 cases, 9 are distinctly different from the remaining 23 cases. Among these 9 cases, 8 companies had established joint programs in fewer than 12 percent of their unionized facilities; whereas the other 23 companies had, on average, established joint programs in 72 percent of their unionized facilities. In the 9th case, the percent of the company's domestic plants unionized was only 36 percent in comparison to an average 90 percent in the other 23 cases. Given these sharp distinctions, the 9 cases identified are included in the Mixed strategy.

Only four companies were reportedly neutral to unionization and indifferent to joint activities. These four companies are excluded from the analyses because their responses do not readily fall into one of the three identified strategies. Finally, two respondents failed to answer both questions and thus are also excluded.

By partitioning headquarter responses as described, 35 percent of the

Chart 3.1
Labor-Relations Strategy Choices
Among U.S. Manufacturing Corporations

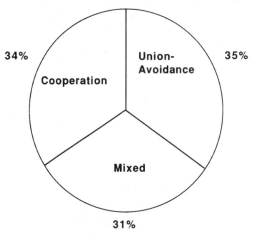

sample of headquarters have chosen to pursue Union-Avoidance strategies, 34 percent Cooperation strategies, and 31 percent Mixed strategies (See chart 3.1). Next, I summarize the results of an empirical study of key factors influencing executive choices of these three grand strategies, conducted with David Meyer and published in the *Industrial and Labor Relations Review* in January 1990 (Cooke and Meyer 1990).

General Propositions About Choice of Strategy

Guided by the general theoretical model developed in chapter 2, executives choosing a grand strategy are expected to weigh the perceived costs and benefits of relying solely on their relative power (as depicted by Union-Avoidance strategies) against the perceived costs and benefits of juxtaposing relative power options and cooperative activities (as depicted by Cooperation or Mixed strategies). Market and structural factors (operational, financial, and extent of union representation) are expected to influence these perceived costs and benefits, and in turn lead corporate executives to choose one grand strategy over the others. Assuming executives act to optimize net benefits to the corporation, it follows that by choosing either a Cooperation or Mixed strategy, executives and union representatives have concluded that, more or less, cooperation yields greater benefits than no cooperation. Among those companies choosing a Union-Avoidance strategy, it follows that executives perceive they will derive greater net gain from relying strictly on their relative power than from juxtaposing relative power options and cooperative activities. Union leaders representing employees in these companies may agree or disagree with that corporate choice. Union leaders, that is, may agree that traditional adversarial relationships are preferred over cooperative relationships. They are unlikely to agree, however, to corporate activities designed to destroy the union, activities that are part and parcel of many aggressive Union-Avoidance strategies.

Among the three grand strategies identified, the Mixed strategy is viewed as the least aggressive. In choosing a Mixed strategy, management needs to find some balance between union avoidance activities on one hand, and cooperation activities on the other. In finding this balance, companies will be less able to act aggressively in pursuing union avoidance activities if simultaneously they are to aggressively pursue cooperation. As aggressive union avoidance activities will be perceived by union leaders as a challenge to the very legitimacy of union representation (Oswald 1986), the contradictory message to union leaders underlying a Mixed strategy becomes less manageable the more aggressive the company's union avoidance activities. One can also imagine that joint activities are less extensive and intensive in plant settings where both plant management and local union leaders perceive that upper management is less than fully committed to cooperation (Boylston 1986).

In comparison to the Mixed strategy, the more aggressive Union-Avoidance and Cooperation strategies are also more risky. Among highly unionized corporations (as in the present sample), an aggressive Union-Avoidance strategy pits the company against its union(s), and unions are not without considerable power to inflict costs on companies for aggressively pursuing Union-Avoidance strategies. Aggressive efforts at cooperation are likewise risky. Until very recently, the parties had very limited experience or expertise at formulating and implementing the significant organizational changes required to make cooperative efforts successful. History also demonstrates that unless the parties find ways to minimize the problems that undermine cooperative efforts (see chapters 5 and 6), these recent efforts will follow the course of American history, a history of short-lived efforts.

Finally, in choosing a grand strategy, it seems reasonable to assume that, in general, executives prefer to manage without unions. Hence, after weighing the potential costs and benefits across the three strategic choices (in light of market pressures and the company's collective bargaining, operational, and financial structures), all factors the same, executives will choose a Union-Avoidance strategy. Indeed, some executives may be willing to accept an unnecessary additional cost merely to satisfy their antiunion ideologies. To the extent they are, the more likely they will choose a Union-Avoidance strategy.

An Empirical Test of Factors Influencing the Choice of Strategies

In order to test hypotheses about financial structure and to control for changes in market conditions, data derived from the Headquarters Executive Survey were merged with financial records of publicly held corporations (provided by COMPUSTAT[12]) and industry data (provided by the U.S. Department of Commerce[13]). Only 90 headquarters surveyed could be matched with corporations listed by COMPUSTAT. Because of missing data on one or more variables in COMPUSTAT, the final sample comprises 58 publicly held corporations.

The time frame selected for predicting the choice among strategies is 1981, a point in time at which unionized corporations were experiencing substantial increases in domestic and global competition and other market pressures demanding substantial adaptation. Although 1981 is not necessarily the year in which all corporations in the sample shaped and embarked upon their grand strategies, the very early 1980s appear to closely approximate the timing of these choices.

In modeling and testing the hypothesized effects of market and various structural factors on the choice of strategies, it is recognized that the choices are not ordered. That is, some factors are expected to influence the choice between the less aggressive, less risky Mixed strategy and one or the other more aggressive, more risky single-approach strategies (Union-Avoidance or Cooperation). While some of these factors, furthermore, are not expected to signal employers that a Union-Avoidance strategy should be preferred over Cooperation (or vice versa), other factors are expected to signal employers to choose Union-Avoidance over Cooperation (or vice versa). An appropriate statistical estimator for testing this kind of discrete unordered choice model is multinomial logit (Amemiya 1981).

Effect of Market Factors on Choice of Strategy

All other factors held constant, it is found that the greater the increase in import penetration (over the 1978 to 1981 period) in the corporation's primary product market, the more likely the corporation chooses a Union-Avoidance strategy over either a Cooperation or Mixed strategy. Given the greater need to be aggressive and risk taking, it can be expected that corporations would choose a Union-Avoidance strategy over a Mixed strategy. It remains unclear, however, why a Union-Avoidance strategy would also be much more preferred than a Cooperation strategy. Perhaps the difference is attributable to management's general preference for managing in nonunion settings.

Another market factor significantly related to choice of strategy is the change in the corporation's industry employment (measured over the 1978-1981 period). The more serious the decline in employment, the more likely corporations chose either Cooperation or Union-Avoidance strategies over Mixed strategies. Again, it is inferred that more serious market threats require more aggressive, riskier strategies.

Extent of Union Representation on Choice of Strategy

The evidence strongly supports the expectation that the more highly unionized the corporation, the less likely Union-Avoidance strategies are pursued. Indeed, the larger the proportion of a corporation's plants unionized, the more likely Cooperation strategies are chosen over either Union-Avoidance or Mixed strategies. These results are consistent with the expectation that the potential disruptive costs associated with Union-

Avoidance activities in highly unionized companies are substantially higher than in companies with lesser union representation.

Effects of Operational and Financial Structures on Choice of Strategy
There is substantial evidence that the choice of strategies is also significantly influenced by a variety of factors reflecting differences in the operational structure and the financial structure or conditions of corporations. First, the higher the average labor cost component of production, the less likely corporations pursue either one of the more aggressive, riskier strategies. This finding is consistent with the expectation that the more labor-intensive the operations, the riskier becomes a Union-Avoidance or Cooperation strategy. Labor's resistance to union avoidance activities, that is, leads to greater disruption costs, the higher the labor-intensiveness. Failure to successfully implement and maintain joint activities across a company's plants, likewise, would lead to greater losses in reorientation and training investments in joint programs, the greater the labor-intensiveness of production. Underlying this latter argument is the presumption that the necessary reorientation and training costs associated with joint programs are greater, since the labor cost component of production is greater.

Second, in weighing the potential costs and benefits of the various grand strategies in light of the labor cost component of production, the overall size of the average investment in plant operations is also evaluated by executives. Here it is hypothesized that the larger the investment in plant operations, the greater becomes the potential loss from failed strategies, since more is put at risk. Hence, everything else the same, larger average investments in plant operations reduces the likelihood that either Union-Avoidance or Cooperation strategies are chosen (and vice versa). Two variables were used to test this hypothesis: average employment per plant and average sales volume per plant. The results of estimation yield evidence that the larger the average sales volume per plant, the more likely corporations choose a less aggressive, more risk averse Mixed strategy over either a Union-Avoidance or Cooperation strategy. Insignificant results are obtained with respect to the effect of average plant size on strategy choice.

It is also found, as would be expected,that the fewer the number of plants companywide, the less likely corporations choose a Mixed strategy. The logic is that the fewer the number of facilities, the more difficult it becomes to effectively manage the contradictory signals of embracing cooperation on one hand while engaging in union avoidance activities on the other.

Finally, strong statistical support is obtained, showing that the tighter the average cost/price squeeze across facilities (measured as cost-of-goods/sales), the more likely corporations choose Cooperation strategies over either Union-Avoidance or Mixed strategies. Joint activities at the plant level are typically designed to identify and resolve production-related problems and to devise ways to improve productivity and quality and to reduce operating costs. As the potential net benefit from cooperative activities rises, therefore (as depicted by higher cost of goods-to-sales ratios), the likelihood of choosing a Cooperation strategy rises.

In summary, the limited statistical analysis reviewed herein strongly suggests that corporations went about choosing among several grand labor relations strategies in the early 1980s. The evidence is strongly consistent with a decisionmaking model, wherein corporate executives have chosen strategies that appear to fit within the competitive pressures of their industries and within their collective bargaining, operational, and financial structures in the early 1980s. In the following section I report how companies went about implementing the three grand strategies.

Implementation of Grand Strategies

Key changes in operational and collective bargaining relationships over the 1975 to 1986 period are reported to highlight several distinct outcomes associated with these strategies. The data presented are based on the 115 headquarter executive responses, and companies are classified by grand strategy by the method described above.

Setting the context for the description of key changes that follows, in 1975 Union-Avoiders on average had 26 plants, of which 68 percent were represented by unions. Cooperators, on average, had 13 plants, of which 90 percent were unionized. Companies pursuing Mixed strategies had, on average, 17 plants in 1975, of which 68 percent were unionized. Over the 1975-1986 period Union-Avoiders, on average, increased the number of plants by roughly 29 percent, whereas companies pursuing Cooperation and Mixed strategies increased the number of plants by roughly 18 percent.

As shown in chart 3.2, there are apparent differences across strategies with respect to changes in the union status of manufacturing plants. Over the 1975 to 1986 period, on average, Union-Avoiders increased the proportion of total plants that are nonunion by 23 percent, whereas Cooperators increased the proportion by only 6 percent and companies pursuing Mixed strategies increased the proportion of plants that are nonunion by 15 percent. Second, with respect to the closure of unionized facilities (chart 3.3), on average, Union-Avoiders closed approxi-

Chart 3.2
Proportional Change in Nonunion
Plants (1975 to 1986) by Strategy

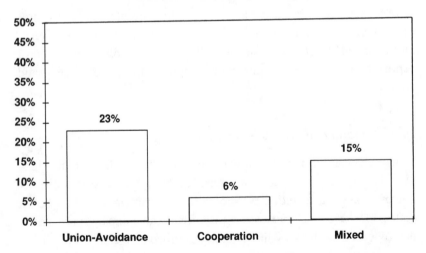

Chart 3.3
Proportion of Unionized Plants Closed
(1975 to 1986) by Strategy

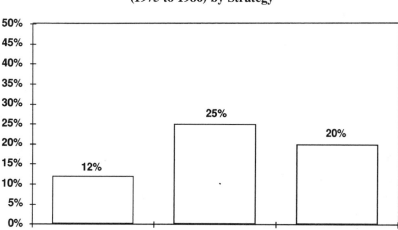

mately 12 percent of their unionized plants over the 1975-1986 period, where in comparison companies pursuing Mixed strategies closed 20 percent and Cooperators closed 25 percent of their unionized plants. Given the figures reported in chart 3.2, although Cooperators closed the largest proportion of unionized plants, they also did not aggressively resist the unionization of plants opened and/or acquired.

A third variable of interest is the extent to which corporations were associated with decertification elections. As reported in chart 3.4, Union-Avoiders were five times as likely to experience decertification elections over the 1981 to 1986 period as were Cooperators (25 percent and 5 percent, respectively). In comparison, companies pursuing Mixed strategies were about three times as likely as Cooperators to experience decertification elections.

Finally, on average, Cooperators had established formalized joint programs (designed to improve company performance and/or quality of

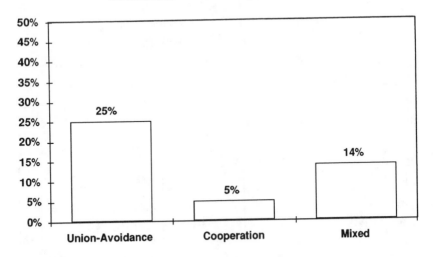

Chart 3.4
Proportion of Corporations Experiencing
Decertification Elections (1975 to 1986)

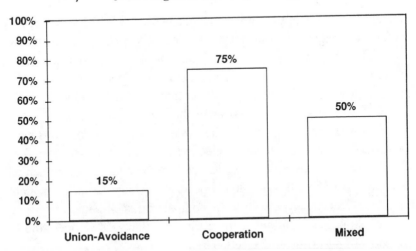

Chart 3.5
Proportion of Unionized Plants With
Joint Programs (1986) by Strategy

worklife) in 75 percent of their unionized plants (chart 3.5). Corporations pursuing Mixed and Union-Avoidance strategies in contrast have
established joint programs in 50 percent and 15 percent, respectively, of
their unionized plants.

In conclusion, the kind of strategic thrusts described herein indicate
that three broadly defined labor relations strategies have evolved over
the last 10 to 15 years. Within these three grand strategies, however,
there is also some notable variation in activities. In particular, within the
Union-Avoidance category, approximately one-third of the companies
did not close any unionized facilities nor experience any decertification
elections. Union avoidance has been restricted apparently to the opening
and/or acquiring of nonunion plants. Within the Cooperation category,
approximately one-third of the companies closed a relatively large
proportion of unionized plants (on average, one-third) and simultaneously opened or acquired a relatively large proportion of nonunion
plants (on average, increasing the proportion of nonunion plants by
about 20 percent). Except for extensive joint activities across their
unionized plants (on average, across 83 percent of their plants), the
strategic changes in these companies look similar to the those observed
for companies in the Mixed category.

Plant-Level Joint Programs
Objectives and Design

Based on the Headquarters Executive Survey, companies pursuing
Cooperation strategies have established joint programs in 75 percent of
their unionized facilities, those pursuing Mixed strategies have established joint programs in 50 percent of their unionized facilities, and even
15 percent of plants parented by Union-Avoiders have established joint
programs. My purpose in this section is to report on the objectives
underlying these joint efforts and on variations and commonalities in
their design.

In both the Plant Manager Survey and Union Officer Survey, respondents were first asked to identify any kind of formalized joint

Table 3.1

Type and Extent of Joint Programs Across Manufacturing

Type of program	Percent of plants with program*
Health and safety committees	48
Quality circles	31
Substance abuse committees	21
Quality of work life/ employee involvement	19
Work teams	18
Productivity committees	17
Labor-management committees	15
Training committees	15
Scanlon or other gainsharing (with employee involvement)	7
Employee stock ownership (with employee involvement)	6
Profit sharing (with employee involvement)	6
Other than above	12

*Based on 194 company responses and 40 unique union responses, N=234

activity that had been established (see questionnaires in appendix). Combining the 194 plant manager responses with 40 unique union officer responses (unique in that no Plant Manager Survey responses were obtained), 54 percent of the 234 facilities represented by these survey responses have embarked on one or more joint programs. Excluding joint health and safety programs (which 48 percent of the sample reportedly have), table 3.1 shows that the most common form of joint activity is the jointly administered quality circle. The least common type of joint program, on the other hand, are programs that tie financial incentives such as gainsharing, profit sharing, and stock

Table 3.2

**Most Important Joint Programs:
Type and Extent**

Type of program	Percent reporting program as most important
Quality circles	31
Labor-management committees	20
Work teams	19
Quality of work life/ employee involvement	15
Productivity committees	8
Scanlon or other gainsharing (with employee involvement)	2
Employee stock ownership (with employee involvement)	2
Other than above	3

N = 129

ownership to employee involvement. Excluding health and safety, substance abuse, and training committees, plants report having, on average, 2.4 different joint programs: 38 percent having one program, 31
percent having two programs, and 31 percent having three or more
programs.

Of course, not all programs survive. Some never get beyond a
memorandum of agreement between the parties; some bloom and then
flounder; others get terminated *de facto* as a result of plant closure. In
the sample of 129 plants that established one or more joint programs, 30
plants (23 percent) reported having terminated one or more joint programs. About 60 percent of these 30 plants, however, continued with or
established other joint programs despite the terminations. Of the 320
joint programs established by the 129 plants in the sample (again
excluding joint health and safety, substance abuse, and apprenticeship
programs), only 35 programs were terminated by 1986. Hence only 11
percent of all joint programs appear to have been terminated.

Objectives and Structure of Joint Programs

In questionnaires sent to both plant-level management and local union leaders, respondents were asked an identical set of questions about the focus and structure of program activities. In the questionnaire to local union leaders, respondents were asked an additional set of related questions. This section first reviews the responses to the first set of questions asked of both parties, and then reviews the responses to questions asked only of local union leaders.

In response to the survey of plant-level management, 111 responses describing joint programs were received. In addition, 18 responses were received from local union leaders describing joint programs for which no plant management response was obtained. These responses are combined to describe programs in 129 different manufacturing plants.

As discussed above, 62 percent of those facilities that have engaged in joint activities have established two or more joint programs. In asking respondents to describe programs and evaluate program success, respondents were asked to answer questions as they would apply to their most important program, where more than one had been established. Table 3.2 reports the type and distribution of joint programs identified by respondents as their most important joint effort.

In asking respondents to describe the focus and structure of their most important joint program, it is found that, in general, team-based programs are very similar in focus and structure – in spite of the categorization reported in table 3.2. Labor-Management Committees (LMCs) and Productivity Committees, on the other hand, appear to have a somewhat different focus and structure than the team-based programs. To facilitate the description of programs, therefore, the sample is divided into two broad categories: (1) team-based programs (quality circles, work teams, QWL/EI, gainsharing, and ESOPs) and (2) committee-based programs (labor-management and productivity committees). As derived from table 3.2, this partitioning of the sample yields 90 team-based programs and 35 committee-based programs that are next described (four programs were not categorizable as either).

Table 3.3

**Team- Versus Committee-based Programs:
Key Problems That Led To and
Are Addressed by Joint Programs**

Key problems	Team-based (N=90) (percent)	Committee-based (N=35) (percent)
Quality of product	49	20
Productivity	33	37
Cost-related	11	3
Labor-management climate	9	29
Absenteeism	8	6
Communications	7	9
Quality of work life	6	3
Job security	6	6
Other	3	14

Primary Focus

Using an open-ended format, respondents were asked to describe the key problems that led to and are addressed by their program. The key problems identified were then categorized, and up to three problems were coded for each respondent. Reported in table 3.3 are the coded responses. Vague responses (e.g., "global competition," "new technology," "changing values of workers," etc.) were coded as "Other."

Among those facilities identifying team-based programs as their most important programs, the most widely cited problems were associated with quality of product (49 percent) and productivity (33 percent). Eleven percent or fewer of the respondents with team-based programs identified any other key problem.

Among those facilities identifying committees as their most important joint efforts, the most widely cited problems addressed by these programs are productivity (37 percent), the labor-management climate (29 percent), and product quality (20 percent). Nine percent or fewer identified any other key problem.

Program Initiation and Start-Up

The great majority of joint programs appear to have been initiated by management (see table 3.4). Approximately 86 percent of key team-based programs and 85 percent of key committee-based programs were

Table 3.4

Initiation and Start-up of Joint Programs

	Percent of team-based programs	Percent of committee-based programs
Program initiated by:		
Company	86	85
Union	4	4
Company and Union	10	11
Year program began:		
Before 1980	11	14
1980	7	3
1981	6	14
1982	16	11
1983	15	23
1984	16	20
1985	24	9
Early 1986	6	6

Table 3.5

Assistance From Outside Organizations

Organization	Not at all (percent)	Some (percent)	Very much (percent)
Industrywide labor-management committee	91	9	-
Areawide labor-management committee	82	15	3
Federal Mediation and Conciliation Service	81	16	3
U.S. Dept. of Labor	81	16	3

initiated by management. Only 4 percent of these key programs were initially promoted by unions.

Also reported in table 3.4 are the years programs began. It is obvious that joint efforts are relatively new, given that 89 percent of the team-based programs and 86 percent of the committee-based programs were established in 1980 or later. Over 50 percent of all programs described were begun between 1983 and 1985.

There are several nonprofit organizations and federal government agencies involved in the promotion of labor-management cooperation. In particular, these include areawide and industrywide Joint Labor-Management Committees (JLMCs), the Federal Mediation and Conciliation Services (FMCS), and the U.S. Department of Labor (Bureau of Labor-Management Relations and Cooperative Programs). Respondents were asked to indicate the extent to which their plant worked with the above "organizations in designing and/or implementing cooperative programs." As reported in table 3.5, the parties have not relied to any substantial degree on either kind of outside JLMC or on either the FMCS or U.S. Department of Labor for assistance in getting started. Only 9 percent of the plants were assisted by industrywide JLMCs, 18 percent by the FMCS, and 19 percent by the U.S. Department of Labor. Overall, however, 33 percent of the plants with joint programs worked at least "some" with one or more of these outside nonprofit agencies.

Formal Structure

Team-Based Programs: Upon examining the formal structures of joint programs, some clear commonalities among team-based programs are found. On average, steering committees that oversee team-based activities consist of five union representatives and five to six management representatives. The most common split is four union and four management representatives. Some steering committees, however, are considerably larger, with up to as many as 12 union and 12 management representatives. In some committees, furthermore, union representation accounted for as little as 5 percent of committee membership, in others as high as 90 percent.

On average, steering committees meet every five weeks, but most commonly every four weeks. Regularly scheduled meetings, however, ranged anywhere from every week to every 16 weeks. The work groups or teams themselves generally meet far more frequently, on average every two weeks. The most common schedule is to meet once every week. In one case, however, teams meet only once every three months.

Committee-Based Programs: The formalized structure of committee-based programs also has strong commonalities across facilities. On average, committees are comprised of seven top union officials and seven to eight company officials. The most common configuration is five to six union and five to six management officials. The largest committee is comprised of 15 union and 15 management officials, while the smallest is comprised of one union official and four managers.

Roughly 50 percent of the committees meet every four weeks. The remaining programs have scheduled meetings ranging from biweekly to 16-week intervals. In addition to the regular committee meetings, approximately 40 percent report having some form of shop-floor team meetings—either as special task groups assigned by the committees or as departmental labor-management or productivity committees. However, in contrast to the team-based programs, for which teams generally meet every week or two, these shop-floor committees meet on average only every four weeks.

Employees Covered in Team-Based Joint Programs

An attempt was made to estimate how widely diffused or extensive joint activities are among bargaining unit employees. Regrettably, the question was apparently stated in such a way that the responses have ambiguous value. Respondents were asked to report "the proportion of bargaining unit employees covered by the program." The responses ranged from 1 percent to 100 percent, with 58 percent responding that all bargaining unit employees were covered by the program described. Respondents apparently interpreted "covered" to mean either (a) the proportion of bargaining unit employees for which the joint program was applicable but not necessarily the proportion of employees who have been actively involved in joint program activities, or (b) the proportion of employees who have been actively involved in joint program activities.

Given the recency of the shift toward joint endeavors, it is highly unlikely that many unionized plants have extended their team-based joint programs to actively involve 100 percent of bargaining unit employees. Assuming that respondents who reported 100 percent coverage did, indeed, misinterpret the intent of the inquiry, some light can be shed on how widely diffused these joint activities are within facilities.

Table 3.6 provides a breakdown of coverage into several categories, both from the original responses and then excluding the 100 percent category. As shown for the latter case, in 56 percent of the plants, between 1 and 25 percent of bargaining unit employees are covered; in 28 percent of the plants, between 26 and 50 percent of employees are covered; and in 16 percent of the plants, between 51 and 99 percent of employees are covered. On average, roughly 21 percent of bargaining unit employees are actively involved in joint program activities. Although the reader must exercise caution with these figures, they provide some tentative evidence that three out of four team-based programs have yet to actively involve a majority of bargaining unit employees.

Additional Union Officer Survey Responses

The survey mailed to union officials asked several questions about the structure and process of joint activities not asked in the survey to plant-level managers. In this section we briefly review these union responses.

Outside Assistance: First, 41 percent of the respondents report that national or regional union offices provided expertise or resources regarding joint activities. The majority, therefore, did not receive any such assistance from the union hierarchy. Second, 47 percent responded that one or more neutral outside consultants were used to help facilitate joint activities in their plants. Approximately 22 percent of the respondents indicated that assistance from both the national or regional offices and outside neutral consultants was used, whereas 33 percent indicate that neither form of outside assistance was utilized.

Union Facilitators: Union officials were asked whether any union representatives had been assigned or elected by the union to act as joint program coordinators or facilitators. About 35 percent responded they had. Of these, 68 percent had one or more full-time joint program facilitators and 32 percent had one or more part-time joint program facilitators. There was no overlap in these two categories; facilitators were either all full time or all part time. The majority of those unions with full-time coordinators or facilitators have one such person, but the

Table 3.6
Proportion of Bargaining Unit Employees Covered
by Team-based Programs

Percent covered	Percent in category (all responses, N=78)	Percent in category (excluding response of 100%, N=33)
1 - 25	23	56
26 - 50	12	28
51 - 75	6	16
100	58	-

Table 3.7

Joint Program Modification of Contract

Extent of change allowed	Wages and benefits (percent)	Work rules (percent)
Not at all	89	63
Very little	6	16
Little	2	14
Much	3	8

number ranges to as high as 18. Those local unions with part-time coordinators or facilitators typically have one or two, but in several cases the locals had eight to ten part-time facilitators.

Attendance Record: According to union respondents, both steering committee meetings and shop-floor meetings are generally well attended. Only 9 percent of respondents indicated that steering committee meetings were poorly attended. Only 2 percent indicated that shop-floor team meetings were poorly attended.

Infringement on Labor Contracts: Finally, several questions were asked addressing the potential overlap or infringement of joint activities on the terms and conditions of the contract. First, respondents were asked to what extent joint teams and committees were allowed to modify either work rules or wages and benefits negotiated in the labor agreement. As reported in table 3.7, 89 percent of the respondents report that joint teams and committees are NOT allowed to modify wages or benefits. In only 3 percent of the programs are participants allowed "much" leeway in altering negotiated wages or benefits. With regard to work rule modification, the parties allow more opportunity to change contractual agreements. Yet even here, little change is generally allowed; 63 percent allow for no modifications and 30 percent allow for very little or little change.

Respondents were further asked to describe the procedures to be followed when proposals for contract modifications are allowed. The standard procedure has two steps: first, the top level steering or labor-management committee of the program must agree to the proposed changes. Second, a majority ratification vote of the bargaining unit must be obtained.

A third question pertinent to the issue of overlap asked, "to what extent do union representatives who serve on the contract negotiation team or who are regular grievance committeemen also serve in key positions in joint program committees?" Roughly 72 percent responded that there was "much" or "very much" overlap; 23 percent reported "very little" overlap. Only 5 percent reported no overlap.

Summary and Conclusion

Based on a survey of company headquarters, executives have very recently fashioned three fairly distinct labor-relations strategies. Among those companies pursuing Cooperation strategies, by 1986 about 75 percent of their unionized manufacturing plants had established formalized joint programs. Among companies pursuing Mixed strategies, about 50 percent of their unionized plants had established formalized joint programs by 1986. Only 15 percent of the unionized plants in which parent companies are pursuing Union-Avoidance strategies have established joint programs. In choosing among these grand strategies, the evidence presented herein implies that executives weighed the perceived effects of market conditions and corporate structural variables on the potential costs and benefits associated with the three grand strategies. In turn, the strategy chosen reflects executives' perceptions about which grand strategy optimizes net gains. Key factors associated with these choices can be summarized as follows.

- The more severe become market conditions (depicted by rising import penetration and declining industry employment), the more likely companies choose either the more aggressive Union-Avoidance or Cooperation strategies over

the Mixed strategy. On net, the choice is most likely to be a
Union-Avoidance strategy.

• The greater the union strength (depicted by percent of
company facilities unionized), the more likely companies
choose a Cooperation strategy over both Union-Avoidance
and Mixed strategies.

• The lower the labor intensity of production (measured by
labor cost/total value ratios and by the average value added
per employee) and the smaller the average plant investment
(proxied by plant sales), the more likely a Union-Avoidance
or Cooperation strategy is chosen over a Mixed strategy, and
the more likely a Union-Avoidance strategy is chosen over a
Cooperation strategy.

• The greater the number of plants, the more likely companies choose a Mixed strategy, with a larger proportion
moving away from choosing a Cooperation strategy than
moving away from choosing a Union-Avoidance strategy.

• The higher the cost-to-sales ratio, the more likely companies choose a Cooperation strategy. As the cost-to-sales
ratio rises, companies move away from choosing a Mixed
strategy but not away from choosing a Union-Avoidance
strategy.

I have also attempted to document the objectives and structure of joint
union-management programs in U.S. manufacturing. Based on a survey
of 350 plant managers and their local union leader counterparts,
roughly one-half of these manufacturing facilities have embarked on
joint programs established to improve plant-level performance and/or
labor-management relations. This figure excludes joint programs on
health and safety, substance abuse, and apprenticeship training. Nearly
all joint programs were begun in the last 10 years; over 50 percent of
programs were begun during the 1983-1985 period. The primary foci or
purposes of these joint programs are enhancing product quality, increasing productivity, and improving labor-management climates.

Joint programs can be categorized reasonably well into two basic types. The first are team-based efforts, in which bargaining unit employees are involved in shop-floor problemsolving (quality circles, work teams, quality of work life/employee involvement, and those employee involvement programs with gainsharing or profit sharing incentives). The second are committee-based efforts, in which plant management and local union leaders are involved in plantwide problemsolving (labor-management or productivity committees). It appears that within plants, the diffusion of team-based activities has yet to involve a majority of hourly employees. One must bear in mind, however, that most joint efforts are relatively new and that expansion of employee involvement activities takes considerable time. It is important to note that only 11 percent of all joint programs established in recent years have been terminated, suggesting that these new cooperative efforts have some durability.

Lest the reader gets the wrong impression, the statistical analysis of the choice to cooperate should be viewed with caution. The analysis is based on a small and unique data base, the information available is limited (potentially leading to incomplete and overly simplified analyses), and the theory underlying any tests of hypotheses is in a formative, incomplete stage and hence, any inferences about causality are tentative.

One can readily surmise, however, that unless cooperative efforts maximize net gains to all parties involved, the parties that have chosen to engage in cooperative activities will ultimately choose to abandon these efforts. Abandonment would be American history repeating itself, except in today's competitive markets the alternative is not yesterday's adversarial relationship of hard-nosed bargaining and contract administration. Today's alternative is to pit unions against employers in an all-out struggle over deunionization.

NOTES

1.   *Economic Report of the President*, 1990, Washington, D.C.: U.S. Government Printing Office, table C-39, p. 338.

2. *Economic Report of the President*, 1990, Washington, D.C.: U.S. Government Printing Office, table C-64, p. 364, and table C-66, p. 70.

3. *Economic Report of the President*, 1990, Washington, D.C.: U.S. Government Printing Office, table C-71, p. 376.

4. *Economic Report of the President*, 1990, Washington, D.C.: U.S. Government Printing Office, table C-109, p. 418.

5. *Annual Energy Review*, U.S. Energy Information Administration, Washington, D.C., U.S. Government Printing Office, various issues.

6. See *Daily Labor Report*, Bureau of National Affairs, No. 18, January 30, 1989, B-13.

7. Comparable figures beyond 1986 are not available. International Trade Administration, U.S. Department of Commerce, unpublished estimates.

8. *Economic Report of the President*, 1990, Washington D.C., U.S. Government Printing Office, table C-21, p. 317.

9. Dataquest, Inc., San Jose, CA, unpublished data.

10. *Economic Report of the President*, 1990, Washington, D.C., Government Printing Office, table C-60, p. 362.

11. See Kochan, McKersie, and Cappelli 1984; Verma 1985; Kochan, Katz, McKersie 1986.

12. Standard and Poor's COMPUSTAT Services, Inc. Data were selected from COMPUSTAT II. Definitions of variables used are provided in *Industrial Compustat*. sec. 9, pp. 27, 33, 38, 48.

13. Import penetration ratios were provided by the Bureau of Industrial Economics. All other industry data were obtained from the Office of Business Analysis, Industry Profile Data Base.

Appendix to Chapter 3

In this appendix are tables pertinent to the analysis of factors affecting corporate choics of labor relations strategies. These tables are reprinted from William N. Cooke and David G. Meyer, "Structural and Market Predictors of Corporate Labor Relations Strategies," published in the *Industrial and Labor Relations Review*, Volume 43, Number 2 (January 1990), pp. 280–293.

Table 3A.1

Variable Construction and Data Sources

Variable	Construction
ΔIMPORT	1981 import penetration ratio minus 1978 import penetration ratio of company's primary 2-digit SIC industry [*Source: Dept. of Commerce industry and import files*]
ΔEMPLOY	((1981-78 total industry employment/1978 total industry employment) * 100), using company's primary 2-digit SIC code [Commerce]
%UNION	Percentage of the company's total domestic manufacturing plants represented by unions in 1975 [author's survey]
LCTV	((Total 1981 industry payroll/(total 1981 shipments) + (total 1981 inventory - 1980 inventory)) * 100), using company's 2-digit SIC code [Commerce]
ADDVALUE	((1981 operating income + (1981 inventory - 1980 inventory))/1981 total company employment) [COMPUSTAT]
PLNTSIZE	Total company employment in 1981/total manufacturing plants in 1975 [COMPUTSTAT: survey]
AVGSALES	Total company sales in 1981/total manufacturing plants in 1975, in millions of dollars [COMPUTSTAT: survey]
NPLANTS	Total number of domestic manufacturing plants in 1975 [survey]
SQUEEZE	((1981 total sales - 1981 operating income)/1981 total sales) [COMPUTSTAT]

Table 3A.2

Means and Standard Deviations (in Parentheses) of Exogenous Variables by Strategy

Variable	Strategy			
	Total sample	Union avoidance	Mixed	Coope-ration
IMPORT	11.27	8.76	12.12	11.72
	(8.93)	(5.09)	(9.46)	(10.84)
ΔIMPORT	1.13	1.424	1.47	.54
	(3.01)	(2.317)	(1.88)	(4.28)
ΔEMPLOY	−13.29	−16.10	−9.88	−14.49
	(16.10)	(17.13)	(12.51)	(18.55)
%UNION	75.49	69.53	66.28	90.23
	(26.82)	(28.31)	(28.34)	(16.83)
LCTV	11.14	10.12	12.29	10.81
	(3.91)	(4.02)	(4.33)	(3.18)
ADDVALUE	24.29	25.60	21.96	25.61
(in $10,000)	(10.45)	(9.12)	(7.93)	(13.48)
PINTSIZE	2240	1650	2895	2052
	(3525)	(2543)	(4584)	(2982)
AVGSALES	407.4	224.1	474.2	493.1
(in $millions)	(537.9)	(207.3)	(618.9)	(621.3)
NPLANTS	17.24	14.12	25.62	11.10
	(22.40)	(16.00)	(31.36)	(11.36)
SQUEEZE	87.91	86.80	86.92	89.89
	(4.67)	(4.09)	(4.29)	(5.06)
N	58	17	21	20

Table 3A.3

Multinomial Logit Estimates of the Odds of Choosing Corporate Strategies

Variable	$\ln(P_{ua}/P_m)$	$\ln(P_c/P_m)$	$\ln(P_c/P_{ua})$
ΔIMPORT	+1.276***	+.445	−.831**
	(.439)	(.289)	(.362)
ΔEMPLOY	−.179***	−.120**	+.058
	(.059)	(.055)	(.045)
%UNION	+.017	+.065**	+.048**
	(.025)	(.029)	(.025)
LCTV	−.860***	−.545**	+.315
	(.256)	(.226)	(.196)
ADDVALUE	+.260***	+.231**	−.028
	(.106)	(.099)	(.058)
PLNTSIZE	−.00009	−.00015	−.00006
	(.00015)	(.00014)	(.00016)
AVGSALES	−.0045**	−.0038**	+.0008
	(.0021)	(.0018)	(.0013)
NPLANTS	−.089**	−.102*	−.013
	(.041)	(.058)	(.047)
SQUEEZE	+.331	+.652***	+.320**
	(.210)	(.227)	(.151)
Intercept	−27.433	−60.099***	−32.667**
	(19.273)	(20.745)	(13.844)

$\chi^2 = 58.842***$,
18   d.f.; N = 58

P_{ua} = the probability of selecting the union avoidance strategy; P_m = the probability of selecting the mixed strategy; P_c = the probability of selecting the cooperation strategy.
*Significant at the .10 level; **significant at the .05 level; ***significant at the .01 level (two-tailed tests).

4

Outcomes Associated With Cooperation

The purpose of this chapter is twofold. First, I report the perceptions of plant-level managers and local union officers regarding changes in company performance, labor relations climates, and outcomes specific to unions and their members. These reported changes, however, apply to perceived changes occurring after the introduction of joint programs and not necessarily as the result of the introduction of joint programs. In the second section, therefore, the theoretical linkage between joint activities and these perceived plant-level outcomes is modeled and findings from several empirical tests are summarized. At a more aggregated level, I then examine the effects of the various grand labor relations strategies on corporate performance.

Perceived Outcomes Associated With
Joint Activities at the Plant Level

In both the Plant Manager Survey and Union Officer Survey respondents were asked: "Comparing the five year period prior to implementation of the most important joint program identified above, please indicate the degree to which the variables identified below have changed." The response categories provided are: much higher, modestly higher, about the same, modestly lower, and much lower. Presented graphically in charts 4.1 through 4.11 are the responses from approximately 110 plant managers and 65 local union leaders who reported having established joint team-based or committee-based programs defined in chapter 3. Responses indicating that the selected outcome had either worsened "modestly" or by "much" are collapsed into one category because very few responses indicated the selected outcomes had worsened by "much." For ease of presentation, the proportion of respondents reporting that the selected outcome was "about the same" are omitted.

In charts 4.1 and 4.2 are the management and union leader reported changes in worker productivity, product quality, and rate of scrappage or waste. In general, it appears that the perceptions of managers and local union leaders are largely consistent with respect to these changes in company performance. At least one-half of the respondents perceived that there have been modest improvements in productivity and quality. A much smaller proportion of managers and union leaders (about 10-20 percent) perceived that there has been much improvement in productivity, quality, and rate of scrappage. Very few respondents (but some) reported that productivity and quality have worsened. One obvious difference in opinion between managers and union leaders is observed in reference to scrappage and waste; 18 percent of the union leaders reported worsening performance, whereas only 4 percent of managers reported worsening performance.

Charts 4.3 and 4.4 report responses to several outcomes related to what might be thought of as labor relations climate variables. Again, the responses across the management and union leader samples are largely consistent. With respect to grievance rates, it appears that in roughly 20 percent of the plants with joint efforts, grievance rates have become much lower, and in approximately 30 percent of the plants, grievance rates have become modestly lower. It appears, however, that in many settings (about one in five) grievance rates are at least modestly higher.

With respect to absenteeism and tardiness, about one-half of the respondents perceive some improvement, most of that being modest. With respect to changes in flexibility of work rules, only about 5 percent report having obtained much greater flexibility after embarking on joint activities, and only about 25 percent report having obtained modestly greater flexibility.

Charts 4.5 through 4.8 summarize responses to several outcomes pertinent to changes in labor-management relations. Direct comparisons of responses between union leaders and plant managers cannot be made here because some questions were worded differently in the

Chart 4.1

Perceived Changes in Company Performance
(Plant Management Response)

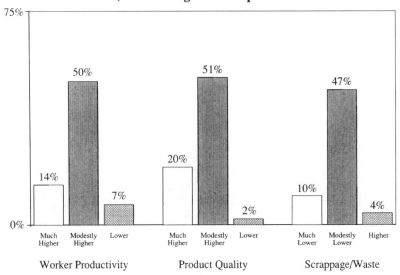

Worker Productivity   Product Quality   Scrappage/Waste

Chart 4.2

Perceived Changes in Company Performance
(Local Union Leader Response)

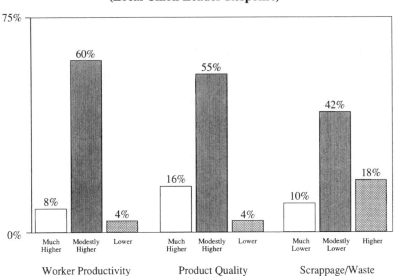

Worker Productivity   Product Quality   Scrappage/Waste

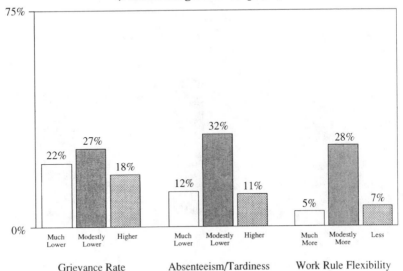

Chart 4.3

**Perceived Changes in Climate
(Plant Management Response)**

Chart 4.4

**Perceived Changes in Climate
(Local Union Leader Response)**

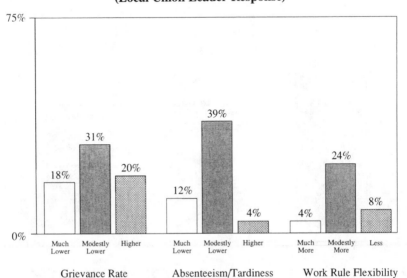

survey instruments to each sample and other questions were asked only of local union leaders. As reported in charts 4.5 and 4.6, it appears that just over 25 percent of respondents perceive that the adversarial or problemsolving relationship between plant managers and union leaders has been much improved. Another 40 percent perceive modest improvement in these relations. Plant-level managers appear to perceive that there has been much greater improvement in reducing adversarial supervisor-worker relationships than do local union leaders. (These reported differences, however, could be attributed to differences in the wording of questions.) It also appears that some parties have been able to capitalize on improved cooperative relations developed through joint efforts when subsequently engaging in contract negotiations. About 15 percent report much improvement in the cooperative spirit at negotiations and another 30 percent report experiencing modest improvement. The difficulty of juxtaposing the more cooperative process of joint activity with the inherently more adversarial process of contract negotiations is highlighted, however, by noting that over 20 percent of the union leaders and 15 percent of the plant managers report that the cooperative spirit of negotiations has worsened since joint activities were begun.

As reported in charts 4.7 and 4.8, a majority of local union leaders report that the parties to cooperative efforts have improved their understanding of each other's interests, objectives, and roles. One-fifth of union leaders report that management's understanding of the union leader roles and interests has been much improved. Another one-third perceive there has been modest improvement. Union leaders also report some improvement in plant management's understanding of worker interests and objectives, with nearly 50 percent of union leaders reporting modest improvement and just over 10 percent reporting much improvement along these lines.

The opposite also appears to be true. That is, (see chart 4.8) in a majority of settings union leaders and members have improved their understanding of management's business interests and objectives. This appears especially to be the case for union leaders, whereby over 20 percent report having a much better understanding and over 50 percent report having a modestly better understanding of management interests.

Chart 4.5

Perceived Changes in Labor-Management Relations
(Plant Management Response)

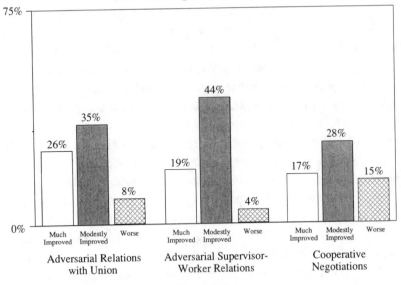

Chart 4.6

Perceived Changes in Labor-Management Relations
(Local Union Leader Response)

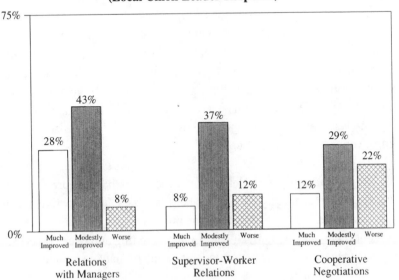

Chart 4.7

**Perceived Changes in Management
Understanding of Union and Worker Interests
(Local Union Leader Response)**

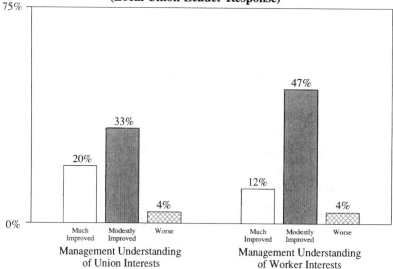

Management Understanding
of Union Interests

Management Understanding
of Worker Interests

Chart 4.8

**Perceived Changes in Union and Worker
Understanding of Management Interests
(Local Union Leader Response)**

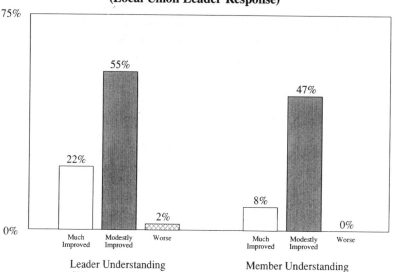

Leader Understanding
of Management Interests

Member Understanding
of Management Interests

Local union leaders were also asked a fairly wide range of questions about potential gains to their members and the union as a whole. As reported in chart 4.9, less than a majority of union leader respondents perceive that member satisfaction with job tasks or work conditions have improved. Most of the improvement, if any, has been modest. A large majority of union leaders, on the other hand, perceived that management has shared more information since the establishment of joint programs (See chart 4.10). Indeed, nearly 30 percent report that much more information has been shared and another 40 percent report that there has been modestly more information shared. In spite of this greater sharing of information, however, it appears that the opportunities for greater union input into business decisions have been relatively limited. Only about 25 percent of the respondents report any greater input after cooperation than before.

Any improvement in the ability of the union leadership to resolve member problems is also a benefit to the leadership. About 10 percent of the union respondents perceive their ability to resolve member problems has become much better; another one out of three leaders report modest improvements. In contrast, approximately 15 percent have found that their ability to resolve member problems has actually lessened.

Finally, several potential gains to the union as an institution are examined. As presented in chart 4.11, unions apparently have not experienced any substantial gains in member commitment to the union. Indeed, only one-third of the union leader respondents reported modest improvement in commitment and nearly one out of five reported commitment has been reduced. On the other side of the coin, however, local union leaders do not perceive companies have gained much higher commitment. Although over 40 percent perceive a modest increase in member commitment to the company, over 20 percent perceive a reduced commitment to the company. Finally, according to local union leader perceptions, the public image of their unions has improved modestly, if at all.

In summary, it is important to emphasize that the reported perceptions above are not attributable to joint activities, but rather merely reflect the perceptions of plant managers and union officers with respect to ob-

Chart 4.9

**Perceived Changes in Quality of Work Life
(Local Union Leader Response)**

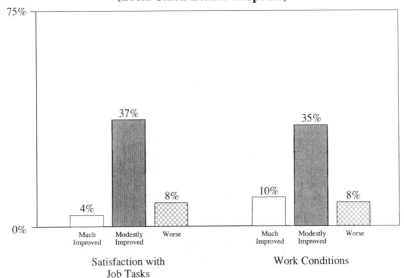

Chart 4.10

**Perceived Gains to Union Leadership
(Local Union Leader Response)**

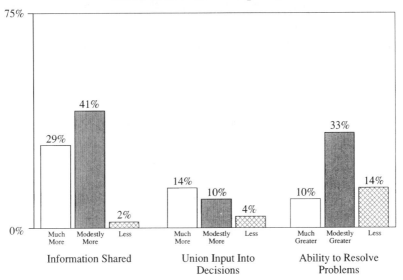

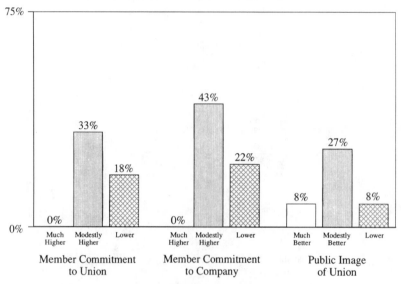

Chart 4.11

**Perceived Gains to Union as an Institution
(Local Union Leader Response)**

served changes since embarking on joint activities. As the theoretical framework presented in chapter 2 highlights, many other factors come into play in cooperative settings that affect these outcomes. My purpose in the next section is to examine the contexts in which cooperation is more or less successful in improving plant performance and labor relations.

Successful Cooperation
Factors That Make a Difference at the Plant Level

Previous Literature

There are a limited number of empirical investigations of cooperative efforts that examine the effects of joint activities across establishments. Schuster (1983) studied nine unionized manufacturing plants to examine productivity and employment levels prior and subsequent to the implementation of gainsharing and joint union-management committees. Based on his interrupted time-series analysis, he finds that, in the short run, in six of eight establishments productivity rose significantly and in eight of nine establishments employment levels remained unaffected after joint activities began. Upon extending his analysis to additional sites, Schuster (1984) found less favorable results. Based on 23 sites, productivity rose in about 50 percent of the sites in the immediate period following the introduction of cooperative programs. In the longer run (up to five years), however, productivity rose in only 17 percent of these sites. Based on a sample of 27 sites, employment remained stable or rose in roughly 80 percent of the sites, in both the immediate period following the introduction of programs and in the longer run.

Voos (1987, 1989) analyzed 350 unionized firms in Wisconsin (1983-1984) and reached the following conclusions:

- All forms of joint programs at the establishment level have positive effects on nearly all performance outcomes (quality, productivity, labor costs, and profits).

- Gainsharing, profit sharing, and employee involvement programs have greater effects on performance outcomes than committee-based programs.

- All forms of joint programs have positive effects on changes in flexibility, absenteeism, and turnover.

- Only general plant committees have consistently positive effects on union leader-management relations, grievance rates, and the ability to resolve grievances informally.

- Profit sharing and employee stock ownership plans have negative effects on union leader-management relations.

Whereas Voos finds that formalized joint activities generally have positive effects, Katz, Kochan, and their co-authors come to the opposite conclusion. In three separate analyses of selected plants represented by the UAW in one American auto company, Katz, Kochan, and others find that QWL and related activities have some very modest effects at best on performance and costs. Katz, Kochan, and Gobeille (1983) conclude that in their sample of 18 plants (1970-1979), more extensive QWL efforts modestly improved quality but had no effect on efficiency. Katz, Kochan, and Weber's (1985) study of 25 plants (1978-1980) leads the authors to conclude that greater QWL involvement had no effect on efficiency and a negative effect on quality. Greater participation in suggestion programs, however, is reported to have positive effects on quality, but still no effect on efficiency. In a more elaborate examination of 53 plants (1979-1986), Katz, Kochan, and Keefe (1987) examine the effects of joint activities on changes in the ratio of supervisors to workers, labor hours in production, and quality. The authors construct composite indices of worker-union participation in group decisions and in technology decisions. The results of their investigation lead the authors to conclude:

- More extensive team-related activities increase labor hours in production and have no effect on either the ratio of supervisors-to-workers or quality.

- Greater worker-union participation in group decisions has no effect on any of the given performance outcomes.

- Greater worker-union participation in technology decisions has generally positive effects on reducing hours of labor for production but inconsistent effects on the ratio of supervisors-to-workers and quality.

In summary, the few studies conducted across plants lead to mixed results with respect to the overall effects of joint programs at the plant level. Although these analyses examine changes in outcome variables within cooperative settings and have to some extent controlled for additional variables expected to affect the outcomes of interest, the authors generally fail to address how other factors in combination with joint activities affect the outcomes of interest.

Next, I examine statistically the importance of a set of key variables expected to influence performance and labor relations outcomes in cooperative settings. First, drawing on the theoretical framework developed in chapter 2, a simplified empirical model of the determinants of cooperative success is presented. Second, the model is operationalized and tested separately with respect to three basic outcomes: perceived changes in product quality, worker productivity, and supervisor – employee relations. These three outcomes are chosen for detailed study because, as reported in chapter 3, they reflect the central foci of joint programs.

Theoretical Model

Guided by the theoretical model presented in chapter 2, it is first assumed that each party to cooperation seeks to find the mix of relative and total power activities that optimizes its own utility. It can be assumed, in turn, that the intensity of joint activities reflects that perceived optimal mix or balance. Central to the analyses that follow is the proposition that the greater the intensity of joint activities at any point in time, the greater the gains derived from those activities at subsequent points in time.

The challenge in identifying important factors that affect the success of joint efforts is the identification of factors that increase the perceived costs or benefits to cooperative efforts. Factors increasing the perceived costs to joint efforts are expected to diminish the intensity of effort and hence degree of improvements. Factors that increase the perceived benefits have the opposite effect on intensity and hence degrees of success.

Based on the available literature and the general theoretical model presented in chapter 2, the outcome model diagrammed in figure 4.1 guides the statistical analyses that follow. The model holds that once joint programs have been established, changes in company performance and labor-management relations in general depend, in large part, on the intensity of joint efforts. Intensity of joint efforts not only has direct effects on performance, but also has indirect effects on performance via any improvements in labor relations. Changes in company performance and labor relations (specifically supervisor-employee relations in the

Figure 4.1

**Model of the Effect of Cooperation on
Performance and Labor-Relations Outcomes**

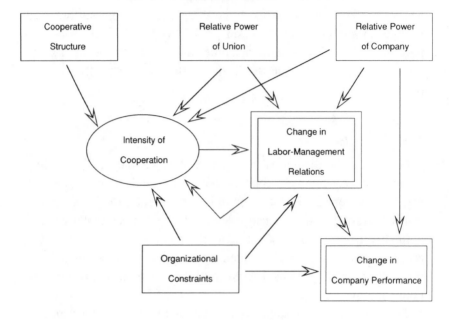

tests that follow) are also directly affected by the relative power of the
union and company and by certain organizational constraints faced by
the parties. Changes in company performance are also affected directly
by the exercise of relative power options available to management.

Central to understanding the analysis herein is the intensity of effort.
Intensity refers to the amount of time, effort, commitment, and the
quality of input applied to joint activities. In part, the level of intensity is
structured. For instance, the larger the proportion of the bargaining unit
employees, the union leadership, and plant management engaged in
joint activities, the more intensive the effort. The literature indicates that
there is enormous variation in these structured levels of involvement.
The more frequently the parties schedule their problem identification
and resolution meetings and the better these meetings are organized or

facilitated, the more intensive the structured joint activities. Intensity, furthermore, is structured in part by the amount, type, and quality of orientation and training undertaken toward developing important technical, team building, and joint decisionmaking skills.

In addition to and within the formalized parameters of joint programs, intensity is conditioned by the level of energy and involvement applied to these efforts by all parties involved. For example, employees may be more or less willing to participate in joint efforts, attend scheduled meetings, or give serious attention to resolving problems or pursuing improvements. As detailed in chapter 5, the greater the extent of problems encountered (e.g., perceived violations of trust or commitment), the less intensive will be cooperative activities. The degree of intensity is also often constrained by various organizational features (e.g., age of workforce, size of facility, and level of resources).

In summary, the simplified model diagrammed in figure 4.1 holds that certain key factors influence performance and labor-relations outcomes in cooperative settings, either directly or indirectly by affecting the intensity of effort. In testing the fundamental propositions underlying the model described, however, it should be borne in mind that the tests conducted do not estimate the separate independent direct and indirect effects, but instead estimate the combined direct and indirect effects of key variables on the selected outcomes. Given limitations of the data collection, it is not possible, furthermore, to test the effect of changes in supervisor-employee relations on changes in company performance. Instead, separate tests are made of the effects of selected variables on the changes in supervisor-employee relations and company performance. In short, in the tests of the model of changes in performance, the effect of changes in labor-management relations are unobserved.

Empirical Tests of Key Factors Influencing Outcomes

The data used for the analyses reported herein are drawn from the Plant Manager Survey responses to the question about the perceived extent of change in quality, productivity, and supervisor-employee relations. Ordered probit estimators are used to estimate the independent effects of selected variables on the outcomes. The rationale underlying the selected hypotheses tested and the results of the estimations are discussed next. A summary of the results is subsequently presented in figures 4.2 through 4.4. (For further details of the statistical analyses, see Cooke 1989a and Cooke 1990.)

Cooperative Structure

With respect to the formalized structure of programs, it is first hypothesized that since team-based programs involve a larger proportion of the workforce and supervision than do committee-based programs, company performance and supervisor-employee relations will improve more under team-based efforts. It is hypothesized, in addition, that the more frequently the parties meet in team-based efforts, the greater the improvements obtained. The results of the statistical tests support the hypothesis (across all three outcomes) that more active team-based programs yield substantially greater improvements than less active team-based programs. Specifically it is found that the likelihood of not obtaining improvements in performance is much greater in team-based programs in which teams are scheduled to meet less frequently than every two weeks than those team-based programs in which teams meet weekly or at least once every two weeks. The same general finding applies to changes in supervisor-employee relations, except that team-based programs in which teams are scheduled to meet weekly are far more likely to yield modest or much improvement in relations than teams meeting less frequently than weekly. From these tests it appears that unless team-based programs call for regular weekly or biweekly meetings, there is very little or no payoff to team-based efforts.

The evidence indicates that committee-based programs are no more effective in improving supervisor-employee relations than team-based programs that schedule meetings less often than weekly. On the other hand, it is found that, on average, committee-based programs have no less effect on quality and productivity improvements than team-based programs in which teams are scheduled to meet at least once every two weeks.

Another factor related to program structure that has a substantial effect on all three outcomes is the extent of union leader participation on top joint steering committees. Where more than six union representatives sit on the top steering committee, the odds of improving quality, productivity, and supervisor-employee relations are considerably greater than when fewer representatives are members of these steering committees. On average, it can be noted that steering committees are comprised of five to six union representatives and five to six managers, albeit the composition of steering committees is fairly wide-ranging. The statistical estimates are consistent with the hypothesis that the more input from union leaders on top steering committees, the greater the intensity of the cooperative effort. That is, greater union leader participation is expected to demonstrate greater support for any team-based or *ad hoc* subcommittee activities on the floor, to provide greater interaction between plant managers and union officials, and in some cases provide active policing of joint activities *vis-a-vis* traditional contract administration.

Consistent with the literature, it is found that the gains from cooperative efforts appear to increase initially, rising at diminishing rates, then eventually falling and leveling off. As reported in numerous cases, there is typically a strong burst of enthusiasm for involvement and participation. However, over time enthusiasm for joint activities wanes, as it does with many new endeavors (Boyle 1986). Second, the identification and resolution of many production and other workplace problems are fairly easy to tackle, but over time become successively more difficult. As gains are harder to accomplish, enthusiasm is harder to maintain, and hence commitment to joint activities often dwindles. Third, over time adversarial conflicts often re-emerge (Hoyer and Huszczo 1988). These events increase distrust between the parties, which only undermines cooperative efforts.

The results of the statistical estimations of this hypothesized relationship between program duration and outcomes are statistically significant with respect to perceived changes in quality and supervisor-employee relations, but not for changes in productivity. Based on the estimates, improvements appear to peak, on average, at about the third to fourth year of program activity.

Union and Management Relative Power

The parties engaged in cooperative activities do not *ipso facto* relinquish the exercise of relative power activities. Instead they must fashion an acceptable balance of relative and cooperative power activities. In choosing to exercise relative power options, the parties must contend with the potential negative effects of that exercise on the labor-management relationship and, in turn, on the intensity of the cooperative effort.

In the statistical estimations, it is clear that, on average, subcontracting out bargaining unit work has a strong negative relationship with changes in quality, productivity, and supervisor-employee relations. It is inferred that this exercise of relative power by management has a serious demoralizing effect on the workforce and union leadership, an effect that reduces the union's commitment to joint activities. Indeed, the likelihood that there is "much" improvement in supervisor-employee relations is reduced by more than 2.5-fold when management subcontracts (every thing else the same). When translated into the effects on performance, the likelihood that there is "much" improvement in quality and productivity is reduced threefold and fivefold, respectively, when management subcontracts.

Although subcontracting out bargaining unit work has very strong negative effects on outcomes, concession bargaining appears to have no effect, on average, on the selected outcomes studied. Nor does technological displacement have a significant effect on changes in product quality or supervisor-employee relations. Technological displacement, however, is significantly associated with improvements in productivity. Here, any negative demoralizing effects on the workforce appear to be offset by the productivity gains associated with new capital investments. As capital investments in plants may be a signal to the union leadership and membership that management is committed to making the plant competitive by allocating resources to capital advancements, one could reasonably conjecture that management's exercise of this relative power option does not carry with it the demoralizing message sent by subcontracting out work.

The economic forces at work that trigger the cooperation more often than not shift the relative power advantage toward management. In the face of management's exercise of the above kind of relative power options in the context of serious competitive threats, unions are hard pressed to exercise their traditional relative power options of striking and slowing down production. As a practical matter, it is difficult to readily identify and measure for statistical purposes the relative power activities of unions in cooperative settings, except as may be inferred (but only in part) by the absence of management's exercise of relative power options. In the present empirical analysis, the percent of production workers represented by unions is used as a rough proxy of a union's relative power (albeit, this is not a fully satisfactory measure of a union's relative power). In any case, it is found that the larger the proportion of employees represented, the more likely there are perceived improvements in quality and productivity. No statistical support is found, however, showing that a larger proportion of employees represented leads to improvements in supervisor-employee relations.

Organizational Features and Constraints

The statistical investigation indicates that there are a number of organizational features and constraints that have independent effects on performance and labor-relations outcomes. First, the evidence indicates that in plants where employment continues to decline, the likelihood that there will be improvements in productivity is diminished. Only very modest support is obtained, however, for continued employment decline reducing the likelihood of obtaining improvements in quality. With respect to changes in supervisor-employee relations, the evidence suggests that where the reduction in force is greater than 25 percent, relations actually improve.

These results are fairly consistent with the hypothesis that continued layoffs have a demoralizing effect on the parties, which diminishes the intensity of the cooperative effort. In the opposite direction, stability or growth in employment has an uplifting effect on the parties, which reinforces the perceived value of cooperative efforts. In the extreme, however, it appears that sharp reductions in employment may have a "shock" effect on the parties, whereby when the very livelihood of the plant is at stake, the parties are shocked into improving relations on the shop floor.

The size of the plant also appears to have an independent effect on outcomes. It is hypothesized that the larger the organization, the less likely improvements in performance and supervisor-employee relations will be obtained. First, the larger the organization, the longer it takes to diffuse cooperative activities across work groups and departments, which, overall, makes cooperative efforts less intensive. Second, the larger the organization, the greater the organizational complexity, making communication and control links more cumbersome to master; all of this reduces intensity of effort. Furthermore, one can imagine that general workforce alienation is greater, the larger the organization, which in turn makes cooperative efforts more difficult to facilitate.

The results of the statistical estimation indicate that all else the same, there is strong statistical support to conclude that it is far more difficult to obtain improvements in productivity and supervisor-employee relations in larger organizations. There is modest support for this conclusion with respect to changes in quality. It is also found, however, that in relatively small plants (fewer than 500 employees), supervisor-employee relations are less likely to improve than in larger plants. This latter finding is consistent with expectation that supervisor-employee relations are generally better to begin with in small *vis-a-vis* medium and large-sized establishments.

Finally, it is often heard that the intensity of cooperative efforts is reduced in establishments employing older, more senior workforces. More senior workers may have more hardened distrustful perceptions about management and, consequently, see less value in cooperating with management. More senior employees, furthermore, enjoying greater job security (via accumulated seniority rights) or facing retirement with accumulated benefits, can be expected to be less enthusiastic about volunteering or participating in joint team-based efforts. Except at the extreme, however, there is reason to believe that greater seniority up to some point increases the intensity of cooperative efforts. First, with greater seniority comes a richer understanding of production problems, and greater skill in devising solutions. Second, more senior employees can be expected to have greater attachment to the place of employment than employees with few years of service. In light of threats of employment loss, employees with greater seniority (but insufficient seniority to protect them from sizable layoffs), can be expected to be more willing to embrace and join in joint activities.

The statistical evidence suggests that indeed, greater average plant seniority, up to 15 years, is associated with greater improvements in supervisor-employee relations. Beyond 15 years, improvements in relations become harder and harder to come by. No statistical support is found, however, to indicate average years of seniority influence improvements in quality or productivity, not even at the extremes.

Summary of Findings

No statistical analyses of human behavior and perceptions have ever proved or disproved any cause-effect relationships. The analysis herein is no exception. Statistical analyses, however, can provide us with more sophisticated forms of evidence upon which to make judgments about important cause-effect relationships. Bearing in mind the many pitfalls and limitations of formulating theory, specifying models of that theory, and empirically testing those models, the statistical analyses herein provide relatively strong evidence that supports a number of common-sense notions about factors that influence the outcomes of cooperative activities. Keeping these caveats in mind, findings of the present empirical investigation are summarized.

To ease the summary, the inferred effects of the variables examined herein on the three major outcomes of interest are presented in figures 4.2 through 4.4. Those variables that on average are associated with greater improvement in a given outcome are listed near the top of each scale. Variables that generally are associated with no perceived improvement or even worse outcomes are listed near the bottom of each scale. Those variables that appear to have no average effect are listed near the middle range of each scale. In reality these latter variables may have positive or negative effects; but if they do, their effects are offset by other unobserved variables not accounted for in the tests.

Figure 4.2

Effect of Selected Variables on Perceived
Changes in Quality

Scale of improvement

• High union leader participation • High percent union representation	**Much improvement (17 percent)**	• Teams meet frequently • Committee-based programs • Program in 3rd or 4th year
• Average seniority (no effect) • Plant size (no effect)	**Modest improvement (49 percent)**	• Technological displacement (no effect) • Concession bargaining (no effect) • Program in 5th year or later
• Continued employment loss • Subcontracting	**About the same (34 percent)**	• Teams meet infrequently • Low union leader participation

Review of the figures highlights a number of tentative conclusions. Note that generally, unless teams in team-based programs meet sufficiently frequently (at least once every two weeks, if not more often) there appear to be no gains. Additionally, note that where union leaders appear to be more actively involved in joint activities and where union representation is more secure or stronger, joint efforts realize greater improvements. At the other end of the scale, it appears that more positive outcomes are harder to come by when management subcontracts out bargaining unit work, where employment levels continue to decline, and in larger manufacturing facilities.

Figure 4.3
Effect of Selected Variables on Perceived
Changes in Productivity

	Scale of improvement	
• High union leader participation	**Much improvement (14 percent)**	• Teams meet frequently • Committee-based programs • Technological displacement
• High percent union representation • Small plants • Average seniority (no effect)	**Modest improvement (48 percent)**	• Concession bargaining (no effect) • Program duration (no effect)
• Continued employment loss	**About the same (31 percent)**	• Large plants • Teams meet infrequently • Low union leader participation
• Subcontracting	**Lower (7 percent)**	

It appears that on average concession bargaining (which typically precedes or accompanies the establishment of joint programs) and technological displacement do not, on net, have strong demoralizing effects on the intensity of cooperative efforts. Last, it appears that positive outcomes derived from joint activities typically peak at about the third or fourth year.

Several general conclusions or lessons can be drawn from this data analysis. First, cooperative efforts can in part be structured to increase intensity of effort, for without sufficient intensity they have no discernable effects on performance or labor relations. Special attention could be

Figure 4.4

**Effect of Selected Variables on Perceived
Changes in Supervisor-Employee Relations**

Scale of improvement

• High union leader participation • Program in 3rd or 4th year	**Much improvement (19 percent)**	• Teams meet frequently • High employment growth • High employment decline
• Low average seniority • Percent union representation (no effect)	**Modest improvement (43 percent)**	• Technological displacement • Concession bargaining (no effect) • Program in 5th year or later
• High average seniority • Subcontracting	**About the same (38 percent)**	• Low union leader participation • Small plants • Very large plants

given to these efforts (typically) in the third or fourth year, in order to infuse greater intensity into the effort. This attention may need to be focused on any demoralizing factors (e.g., growing distrust or factors negatively influencing perceived commitment), and/or on enhancing the problem identification and resolution skills of the workforce.

Another general lesson is that the success of cooperative efforts are dependent on union leader endorsement and participation. To secure or enhance this union leader involvement, the union must be viewed as relatively strong and secure.

Management practices that undermine this involvement, likewise, undermine the potential success of cooperative efforts.

The evidence suggests that the parties in general can juxtapose some forms of relative power activities with cooperative activities (e.g., concession bargaining and technological displacement). Special attention must be paid, however, to the demoralizing effect of subcontracting bargaining unit work. Unless the union leadership and membership can see its justification in light of serious competitive threats and a joint process is established to justify any subcontracting, employers are bound to undermine joint activities by engaging in subcontracting.

Finally, there appear to be factors that are not in the direct control of the parties, but which, when confronted, require special attention. These factors include the continued decline in employment and the organizational constraints of managing in large establishments and where the age or seniority of the workforce is relatively high.

Performance Outcomes Associated With Corporate Strategies

This section summarizes the results of an investigation of the effects of corporate strategies on financial performance (see Meyer and Cooke 1990 for a detailed report). In particular, the independent effects of the competitive restructuring activities reviewed in chapter 3 (the extent of joint programs across plants, the acquisition and/or opening of non-union plants, the closure of unionized plants, and the decertification of unions) on changes in return-on-sales and average added value per employee are estimated. These estimates are made in light of differences in industry market conditions and several other contextual factors across the three grand strategies identified in chapter 3: Union-Avoidance, Cooperation, and Mixed.

Empirical Investigation

As illustrated in figure 4.5, the objective of the investigation has been to account for any changes in performance between 1974-1975 and 1984-1985 attributable to four key strategic labor-relations options identified. In performing this analysis, the independent effect of each of

Figure 4.5

**Corporate Performance as a Function
of Strategic Choices
Options**

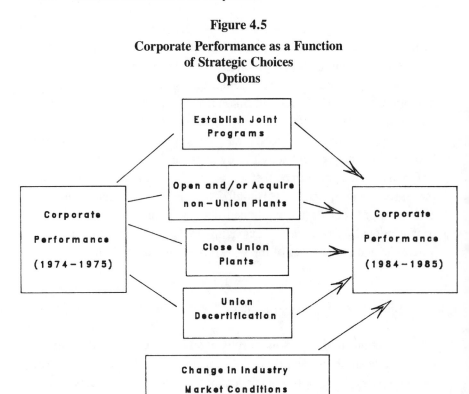

the strategic options on changes in performance is estimated. Additionally, the cumulative effect of various mixes of options chosen on changes in performance is estimated.

Because of limitations on the availability of financial data, the statistical tests are made against a subsample of 56 corporations from the original sample of 115 headquarters. Ordinary least squares regression was used to estimate the effects of the restructuring options on changes in performance. The performance indices are percent change in return-on-sales (calculated as operating income divided by sales) and percent change in added value per employee (calculated as operating income plus inventory, divided by number of employees).

One cannot predict, *a priori*, which of the various restructuring activities or which combination of activities will yield the greatest performance improvements. As discussed in chapter 3, the parties appear to have chosen strategies expected to optimize performance given their specific financial, operational, and collective bargaining structures, as well as market constraints. There are many unknowns, however, about the potential costs, benefits, and risks associated with each strategy. In particular, the degree of union retaliation to various union-avoidance and deunionization activities and the costs incurred therefrom would be difficult to accurately predict. The same can be said about the returns to joint efforts at the plant level. Hence, instead of testing hypotheses about the effect of chosen strategies, Meyer and Cooke attempt to simply estimate effects using a before-after analysis.

The results of the estimations can be summarized as follows:

- The greater the extent of nonunion plants opened and/or acquired, the greater the increase in return-on-sales. Changes in added value per employee appear unaffected.

- The greater the extent of unionized plants closed, the greater the decrease in return-on-sales. Changes in added value per employee appear unaffected.

- Decertification activity reduces return-on-sales and added value per employee.

- Where joint programs have been established in a majority of unionized plants, both return-on-sales and added value per employee increase.

The results of estimation additionally indicate that market conditions have a significant bearing on performance outcomes. The greater the increase or less the decrease in value of domestic industry shipments over the 1975-1985 period, the greater the improvement in return-on-sales and added value per employee. The more severe the increase in import penetration in a corporation's primary industry, the greater the reduction in return-on-sales and added value per employee.

Although Meyer and Cooke do not provide estimates of the average overall gain or loss associated with the three grand labor relations

Table 4.1

Estimated Cumulative Effects of Strategic
Activities on Performance by Grand Strategy
(1974-1975 to 1984-1985)

Strategy	Percent change in return-on-sales	Percent change in added value per employee (nominal $)
Union-Avoidance	.52	-15.1
Cooperation	1.39	18.6
Mixed	.57	1.7

Note: Estimates derived from data provided in Meyer and Cooke (1990).

strategies, here I estimate the cumulative or combined net effect of the identified strategic activities (i.e., extent of joint programs across plants, the acquisition and/or opening of nonunion plants, the closure of unionized plants, and decertification of unions) on company performance. The average cumulative net effects of the various bundles of activities on changes in return-on-sales and added value per employee are reported in table 4.1.

These estimates indicate that Cooperators have gained, on average, the most from their efforts. The change in return-on-sales rose 1.4 percent and the change in added value per employee (using nominal dollars) rose approximately 19 percent over the 1974-75 to 1984-85 period. Union-Avoiders, on the other hand, gained the least from their efforts, on average, increasing return-on-sales by .5 percent and reducing added value per employee by 15 percent. In comparison, those corporations pursuing Mixed strategies increased return-on-sales by .6 percent and added value per employee by 1.7 percent.

Implications and Conclusions

The statistical analysis performed on this small sample of highly unionized manufacturing corporations implies that overall (and only on average), Cooperators have to date gained more from their strategy choice than either the Union-Avoiders or those corporations pursuing Mixed strategies. The estimated gains, however, must be put in a broader perspective. First, the estimated changes in return-on-sales and added value per employee attributable to any combination of the restructuring activities are very modest, indeed. Second, although the Cooperators appear to have gained the most with respect to improvements in return-on-sales, as of 1984-1985 they still reported having the lowest return-on-sales at about 10.75 percent, whereas return-on-sales was just over 11 percent for Union-Avoiders and 13.5 percent for corporations pursuing Mixed Strategies. On the other hand, Cooperators report having the highest added value per employee in 1984-1985 at nearly $33 in comparison to roughly $25 for corporations pursuing either Union-Avoidance or Mixed strategies.

Third, along these lines it must be recognized that the analysis examines only two indices of performance. Indices of financial performance are chosen because the kinds of restructuring activities examined are designed largely to improve production efficiencies and product quality and reduce labor costs. These factors of production have an obvious bearing on the cost-price ratios of production and consequently on profitability derived from sales. These performance measures, however, provide only a partial picture of overall corporate performance. Other measures of performance utilized by executives include market-to-book ratios, return on equity, and return on assets. In the only other published report that begins to address the effects of cooperative strategies on companywide financial performance, the authors conclude that in highly unionized companies, employee involvement programs actually reduce return-on-assets (Delaney, Ichniowski, and Lewin 1988).

Finally, it is doubtful that the 10-year period examined reflects long-run equilibrium. The anticipated gains of the Union-Avoiders may simply require a longer time period in which returns to their strategy are realized. That is, one could argue that the average 20 percent reduction in union coverage of plants among Union-Avoiders is still insufficient to extract the expected gains from deunionization. On average, 50 percent of the Union-Avoiders' plants are still represented by unions. How well will these corporations fare if, over the next 10-year period, union representation is reduced another 20 percent or more?

Add to this that American history clearly highlights the short-lived endurance of cooperative efforts, presumably because the costs outweigh the benefits to at least one party or the other. The limited evidence indicates that the gains from joint efforts peak at the third or fourth year and then slide downward. Applied in the present context, the performance improvements observed by 1984-1985 may, on average, reflect peak performance derived from cooperation. One can surmise that unless these gains can at least be maintained (if not improved upon) over the next 10 years, Cooperators could easily lose any short-term differential they enjoy over Union-Avoiders.

Cooperative Outcomes in Perspective

One anonymous labor-relations executive of a company that touts its new partnerships with unions recently commented to me that "there have been a lot of first-base hits and very few home runs." That sobering statement from an experienced advocate of cooperation is consistent with the investigation presented herein. In general, joint activities have had modest but important effects on labor-management relations and performance. Many exceptions, of course, exist.

The few other empirical studies (those that go beyond specific case analyses) yield mixed results that generally support this conclusion. Unlike most of these other investigations, the analysis presented herein has sought to examine the factors that influence the intensity of effort, and in turn the effects of joint efforts on selected performance and labor relations outcomes. The evidence indicates that there needs to be a certain level of intensity to obtain substantial improvements. This intensity can in part be structured but in part is moderated by other contextual factors and the exercise of relative power. Without sufficient effort to reduce the influence of factors that reduce intensity, it is likely that the parties will continue to bat only first-base hits. Unless these first-base hits translate into a lot of runs, the Cooperators' score card could prove disappointing. It is in this sobering light that key problems undermining the intensity of cooperative efforts are discussed in chapter 5 and prescriptions for success are proposed in chapter 6.

Appendix to Chapter 4

Provided in this appendix are variable definitions, descriptive statistics, and the results of the estimations of the models of perceived changes in productivity, quality, and employee-supervisor relations. These results have been published elsewhere as cited.

Appendix 4A

Reprinted from: William N. Cooke, "Improving Productivity and Quality Through Collaboration," *Industrial Relations*, Vol. 28, No. 2, Spring, 1989: pp. 299-319.

Table 4A.1

Variable Definitions

Variable	Definition
Change in Productivity	Perceived change in productivity per unit of labor. Equals 0 if "modestly lower," 1 if "about the same," 2 if "modestly higher," and 3 if "much higher."
Change in Quality	Perceived change in product quality. Equals 0 if "modestly lower" or "about the same," 1 if "modestly higher," and 2 if "much higher."
Committee-Based Program	Equals 1 if key joint program is a labor-management or productivity committee, 0 otherwise.
Less Active Teams	Equals 1 if key joint program is a team-based program and teams regularly meet less often than once every two weeks, 0 otherwise.

Benchmark category for both Committee-Based Program and Less Active Teams includes team-based joint programs in which teams meet once every one or two weeks.

Leaders on Steering Committee	Equals 1 if more than 5 union representatives sit on top steering committee, 0 otherwise.
Steering Committee Make-up Unknown	Equals 1 if number of union representatives sitting on top steering committee is not reported, 0 otherwise.
Multiple Programs	Equals 1 if more than one joint program exists, 0 otherwise.
Program Duration	1987-year program activities began.

Program Duration^z	Equals log(Z) when X ⟩ Program Duration, equals − (log(Z)) when X ⟨ Program Duration, and equals 0 when X = Program Duration; where Z = 1 + abs. ((X − Program Duration)/(X/ Program Duration)).
Technological Displacement	Equals 1 if respondent reports that since 1975 any "bargaining unit employees have lost their jobs in the plant because of the introduction of new technologies or automation," 0 otherwise.
Subcontracting	Equals 1 if respondent reports that since 1975 the "proportion of bargaining unit jobs [that] have been subcontracted out on a permanent basis" has been either "modest" or "substantial," 0 otherwise.
Concession Bargaining	Number of negotiations since 1975 that respondent characterizes as "concession bargaining (i.e., wage or benefit freezes or cutbacks, elimination of restrictive work rules, etc.)."
Percent Union	Percent of production workers under the identified union contract.
Layoffs	Equals 1 if average plant employment in 1983, 1985 is less than average plant employment in 1979, 1980, 1981; 0 otherwise.
Plant Size	Average size of plant during 1983, 1985.
Average Years	Average length of employment within bargaining unit.
Average Years^z	Equals log(Z) when X ⟩ Average Years, equals − (log(Z)) when X ⟨ Average Years, and equals 0 when X = Average Years; where Z = 1 + abs. ((X − Average Years)/(X/Average Years)).
Percent Female	Percent of bargaining unit employees that are female.

Table 4A.2

DESCRIPTIVE STATISTICS

Variable	Mean or Proportion	S.D.	Range
Change in Productivity			
@ 0	.07	–	–
@ 1	.31	–	–
@ 2	.48	–	–
@ 3	.14	–	–
Change in Quality			
@ 0	.34	–	–
@ 1	.49	–	–
@ 2	.17	–	–
Committee-Based Program	.28	.45	0-1
Less Active Teams	.37	.49	0-1
Leaders on Steering Committee	.28	.45	0-1
Multiple Programs	.73	.45	0-1
Program Duration	5.03	5.13	1-33
Program Duration^z	.75	.92	-4.43-1.10
Technological Displacement	.45	.50	0-1
Subcontracting	.40	.49	0-1
Concession Bargaining	1.17	.88	0-3
Percent Union	95.28	10.64	48-100
Layoffs	.52	.50	0-1
Plant Size	2376	3323	13-24000
Average Years	16.10	5.52	3-32
Average Years^z	1.88	.54	-1.46-2.11
Percent Female	22.80	21.92	0-85

Table 4A.3

ORDERED PROBIT ESTIMATES
(Standard Errors in Parentheses)

Exogenous Variables	Dependent Variables Change in Productivity	Change in Quality
Committee-Based Program	.057	.205
	(.362)	(.392)
Less Active Teams	-.838**	-.831***
	(.348)	(.363)
Leaders on Steering Committee	.899***	1.030***
	(.404)	(.354)
Steering Committee Make-up Unknown	.231	-.732
	(.579)	(.642)
Multiple Programs	.327	.777**
	(.368)	(.424)
Program Duration^z	.199	.402**
	(.179)	(.172)
Technological Displacement	1.079***	.147
	(.367)	(.333)
Subcontracting	-1.092***	-.924**
	(.381)	(.418)
Concession Bargaining	.299	-.060
	(.229)	(.211)
Percent Union	.025*	.051***
	(.015)	(.018)
Layoffs	-.954***	-.604**
	(.347)	(.354)
Plant Size	-.0001***	-.0001
	(.00004)	(.00007)
Average Years^z	-.087	-.694
	(.337)	(.656)
Percent Female	.018**	.008
	(.008)	(.007)
Intercept	-.466	-3.047*
	(1.694)	(1.876)
Mu(1)	0	0
Mu(2)	1.713***	1.926***
	(.351)	(.364)
Mu(3)	3.899***	–
	(.491)	
Log-Likelihood	-73.531	-66.056
χ^2(14 d.f.)	56.928***	43.527***
N	87	86

*** = significant ≤ .01 level, ** = significant ≤ .05 level, and * = significant at < .10 level; using two-tailed tests for all variables except Less Active Teams, Leaders on Steering Committee, Multiple Programs, and Layoffs where one-tailed tests are appropriate.

Appendix 4B

Reprinted from: William N. Cooke, "Factors Influencing the Effect of Joint Union-Management Programs on Employee-Supervisor Relations," *Industrial and Labor Relations Review*, Vol. 43, No. 5, July, 1990, pp. 587-603.

Table 4B.1

Variable Definitions

Variable	Definitions
ΔRELATIONS	Perceived change in adversarial relationship between supervisors and workforce. Equals 0 if "modestly higher" or "about the same"; 1 if "modestly lower," and 2 if "much lower."
ACTIVE TEAMS	Equals 1 if joint program is team-based and teams regularly meet weekly, 0 otherwise.
COMMITTEES	Equals 1 if joint program is committee-based, 0 otherwise.
	Benchmark category for both ACTIVE TEAMS and COMMITTEES includes team-based programs in which teams regularly meet less often than weekly.
LEADERS-ON-STEERING COMMITTEE	Equals 1 if more than 6 union representatives sit on top steering committee, 0 otherwise.
PROGRAM DURATION	1987-year program activities began.
PROGRAM DURATION^z	Equals $\log(z)$ when $X >$ PROGRAM DURATION; equals $-(\log(z))$ when $X <$ PROGRAM DURATION; and equals 0 when $X =$ PROGRAM DURATION; where $z = 1 + \text{abs}((X - \text{PROGRAM DURATION}) / (X/ \text{PROGRAM DURATION}))$.
TECH DISPLACEMENT	Equals 1 if respondent reports that since 1975 any "bargaining unit employees have lost their jobs in the plant because of the introduction of new technologies or automation"; 0 otherwise.

118

SUBCONTRACT	Equals 1 if respondent reports that since 1975 the "proportion of bargaining unit jobs [that] have been subcontracted out on a permanent basis" has been either "modest" or "substantial"; 0 otherwise.
CONCESS1	Equals 1 if since 1975 respondent characterized one round of negotiations as "concession bargaining" (i.e., wage or benefit freezes or cutbacks, elimination of restrictive work rules, etc.)"; 0 otherwise.
CONCESS2	Equals 1 if since 1975 respondent characterized two or more rounds of negotiations as "concession bargaining"; 0 otherwise.
%UNION	Percent of production employees under the identified union contract.
HIGH GROWTH	Equals 1 if average plant employment in 1983, 1985 is 25% higher than average plant employment in 1979, 1980, 1981; 0 otherwise.
HIGH DECLINE	Equals 1 if average plant employment in 1983, 1985 is 25% lower than average plant employment in 1979, 1980, 1981; 0 otherwise.
AVG SENIORITY	Average length of employment within bargaining unit.
SMALL	Equals 1 when average size of plant during 1983, 1985 $<$ 500; 0 otherwise.
LARGE	Equals 1 when average size of plant during 1983, 1985 $>$ 3500; 0 otherwise.

Table 4B.2

Ordered Probit Estimates of Perceived Changes
in Employee-Supervisor Relations
(Standard Errors in Parentheses)

Exogenous Variables	Coefficients and Stnd. Errors	Mean or Proportion
ACTIVE TEAMS	.664**	.34
	(.355)	
COMMITTEES	-.116	.26
	(.401)	
LEADERS-ON-STEERING COMM	.884**	.18
	(.432)	
PROGRAM DURATION^z	.314**	.98
	(.158)	
TECH DISPLACEMENT	-.097	.45
	(.324)	
SUBCONTRACT	-.653**	.40
	(.344)	
CONCESS1	.077	.42
	(.385)	
CONCESS2	.676	.32
	(.456)	
%UNION	.003	95.29
	(.016)	
HIGH GROWTH	1.499**	.12
	(.591)	
HIGH DECLINE	.827**	.31
	(.375)	
AVG SENIORITY	.224***	15.90
	(.087)	
AVG SENIORITY^2	-.008***	287.30
	(.003)	
SMALL	-.851**	.23
	(.383)	
LARGE	-1.447*	.14
	(.668)	
INTERCEPT	-1.839	
	(1.586)	
Mu(1)	0	
Mu(2)	1.695***	
	(.267)	
Log-likelihood	-72.706	
χ^2 (15 d.f.)	46.283***	
N	92	

Dependent variable is ΔRELATIONS, with the following ordered categories and proportion of outcome represented by each category: 0 = about the same or modestly higher (38%); 1 = modestly lower (43%); 2 = much lower (18%).

*** = significant ≤ .01 level, ** = significant ≤ .05 level; * = significant ≤ .10 level; using two-tailed tests for all variables except ACTIVE TEAMS, SUBCONTRACT and LEADERS-ON-STEERING COMM, where one-tailed tests are appropriate.

5

Key Problems Encountered

As synthesized in chapter 1, the literature and testimony identify several fundamental problems encountered in the process of establishing and maintaining good relationships necessary for cooperation. These problems are:

- Distrust
- Lack of Commitment
- Demoralization from Gains Not Gotten
- Juxtaposing Cooperation and Traditional Collective Bargaining

Distrust

Distrust between the parties inhibits the establishment of joint programs. Because distrust between employers and unions often has deep roots, however, the establishment of joint programs typically only signals that the parties are willing to experiment with joint programs. Existing literature and testimony make it clear that joint efforts reflect fairly uneasy partnerships in joint problemsolving. The widely shared conclusion of the literature and testimony is that sufficient trust must be developed over time, else joint efforts will wane and ultimately be undermined by distrust.

Trust is a "firm belief or confidence in the honesty, integrity, reliability, justice, etc. of another person or thing." To trust another party, moreover, means allowing them "to do something without fear of the outcome" (Webster's New World Dictionary 1968). In the context of union-management cooperation, the parties typically ask on a day-to-day basis the following kind of questions in making their assessments of the level of trust that exists between them.

- Do you consult with me?
- Do you share pertinent information, avoiding surprises?
- Are you straightforward and honest with me, relinquishing hidden agendas?
- Do you listen to my opinions?
- Do you follow through with joint decisions and any promises?
- Are you consistent and reliable in your actions?
- Do you forego using double standards for managers and employees?
- Do you forego using threats?
- Do you forego "cutting deals" on the side that are inconsistent with cooperation?
- Do you forego intentionally undermining my role and responsibilities?
- Do you accept unintended failures?
- Do you live up to your role and responsibilities?

When answers to the above questions are answered in the negative, trust is diminished. The more negative the response, the more trust is diminished. As trust is diminished, the parties are unable to develop relationships that maximize the potential benefits of cooperation. Instead, distrust merely increases the potential costs of cooperation, and the intensity of effort applied to cooperative activities is diminished. Serious violations of trust, furthermore, are apt to cause cooperative efforts to be put on hold, if not destroy them altogether.

To examine the perceived magnitude of distrust as a problem, charts 5.1 and 5.2 report the responses of both plant managers and local union leaders to several questions pertinent to the issue of trust. Respondents to the Plant Manager Survey and Union Officer Survey were asked: "To

Chart 5.1

Lack of
Sufficient Trust Between Parties

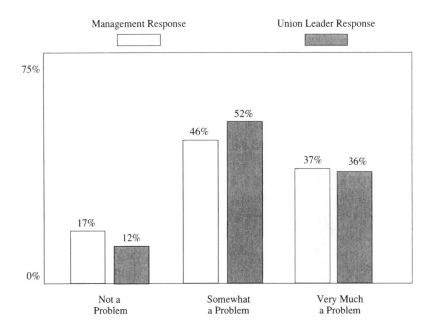

Management Response   Union Leader Response

what extent have the following problems affected the successful implementation and maintenance of your most important joint program...?" Respondents were given a choice of four answers: not a problem, somewhat a problem, very much a problem, or important factor in termination of program. For the sake of simplicity, those few responses that the given problem was an "important factor in termination of program" are included in the charts under "very much" a problem. The responses reported throughout this chapter are drawn from approximately 110 plant manager questionnaires and 60 union officer questionnaires.

Chart 5.1 reports the responses with respect to the extent to which

Chart 5.2

Trust: Violations, manipulation, Cooptation
(Union Response)

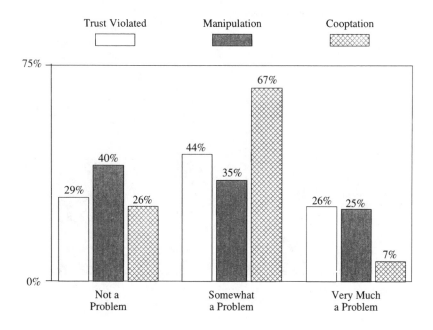

"lack of sufficient trust between parties" is a problem. There appears to be close agreement as to the extent of the trust problem between managers and local union leaders. Only about 15 percent do not find trust to be a problem, whereas about 50 percent find it to be somewhat a problem and roughly 35 percent find it to be very much of a problem.

Chart 5.2 reports the proportion of union leader responses to several trust-related questions. (These problems were not raised in the survey to managers.) The first question asked the extent to which "violation of trust by either party" is a problem. About 45 percent find it to be somewhat of a problem and another 25 percent find it to be very much a problem. The second question asked the extent to which "perceived manipulation of program (or bonus formula) by management" was a problem. Here, about 35 percent find perceived manipulation to be somewhat of a problem and 25 percent find it to be very much a problem. The literature indicates that union leaders often fear that cooperation with management will be perceived by union members as a form of cooptation. Union leaders, of course, want their members to trust that the leadership has in mind the best interests of the membership upon embarking on joint endeavors. To address this dimension of trust, union leaders were asked the extent to which "perceptions by workers that the union leadership has been coopted by management" was a problem. Over 65 percent report that perceptions of cooptation are somewhat of a problem, but only 7 percent find it to be very much a problem.

One aspect of trust focuses on how much trust the union has in management's capabilities to manage the company well. Since skepticism of management's abilities to manage is also likely to be a problem for some organizations, union leaders were asked the extent to which the "local union leadership trust management's capabilities to manage this company." Approximately 21 percent reported "very little," 47 percent reported "little," 22 percent reported "much," and only 10 percent reported "very much."

In summary, the responses to several questions pertinent to trust clearly support the conclusion that the lack of trust is a widespread problem. For a large majority of the parties involved in team-based and committee-based joint programs, distrust is at least somewhat a problem.

Commitment

To "commit" to something means to obligate or bind to some course of action. In the case of union-management cooperation, commitment means to obligate to joint decisionmaking. This commitment, however, is not necessarily to a given program or set of decisionmaking parameters (e.g., to a quality control circle program, where team members meet every week and report to a joint steering committee comprised of five union and five management representatives), but rather to the general process of joint problem identification and resolution. Bear in mind, on the other hand, that in practice the parties may characterize or address commitment in the form of a given joint program structure or set of activities.

There appear to be a number of questions asked by the parties on a day-to-day basis, answers to which help formulate their perceptions about the level of commitment to joint decisionmaking.

- Are you willing to commit time and resources to cooperation?
- Are you willing to work hard at this new process?
- Are you interested in obtaining gains for the other party as well as selfish gains?
- Do you see this process as a long-run effort?
- Are you willing to take political risks in supporting and soliciting support for cooperation?
- Are you willing to assist the other party with his/her organizational and personal political constraints?
- Are you willing to reward subordinates who actively support and engage in joint activities?
- Are you willing to share authority?
- Are you willing to share responsibility for failures and recognition for successes?

When answers to the above kind of questions are answered in the negative, perceptions of lack of commitment arise. The more negative the responses, the more negative the perceptions of commitment. These perceptions may be formulated about the representatives of the other party, or about representatives of one's own organization. The result, in either case, is (again) diminished effort at effective cooperation.

In the survey to local managers and union leaders, respondents were asked a number of questions about the extent to which various dimen-

Chart 5.3

Upper Management Commitment to Joint Programs

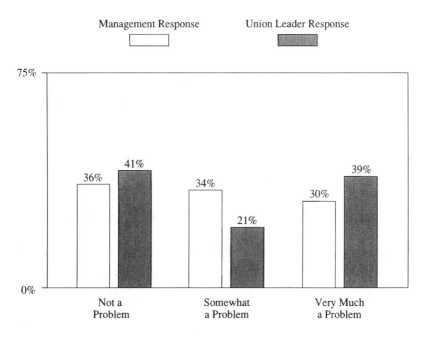

sions of the lack of commitment was a problem. Charts 5.3 and 5.4 report these responses about the extent that "lack of commitment by upper management" and "lack of broad commitment among plant managers," respectively, were problems affecting the success of joint programs. Chart 5.5 reports responses about the extent that "lack of broad commitment by union leaders" was a problem.

As shown in chart 5.3, a majority of both plant managers and local union leaders find that the lack of upper management commitment to joint programs is a problem. Indeed, just under one-third of managers and just over one-third of union leaders perceive the lack of upper management commitment to be very much a problem. With regard to plant-level management commitment (chart 5.4), there is substantial disparity between management perceptions and union leader perceptions. In particular, note that only 17 percent of managers perceive that the lack of broad commitment among plant managers is very much a problem. In sharp contrast, 37 percent of union leaders perceive plant management commitment to be very problematic.

These perceptions of commitment are reversed when the parties are asked about the lack of broad union leader commitment. As reported in chart 5.5, nearly 80 percent of managers report union leader commitment to joint programs as a problem, whereas only 50 percent of union leaders report union leader commitment as a problem. Although, over-

Chart 5.4

Plant Management Commitment to Joint Programs

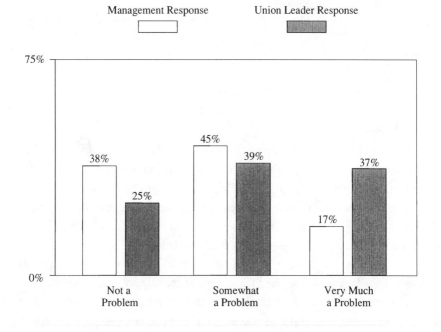

Chart 5.5

Union Leader Commitment to Joint Programs

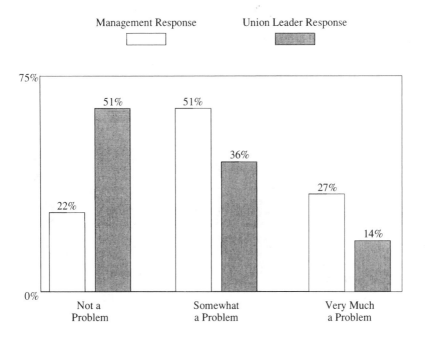

Management Response   Union Leader Response

all, local union leader commitment seems to be a less serious problem than broad plant management commitment, 27 percent of managers find union leader commitment to be very much of problem, whereas 14 percent of local union leaders report union commitment to be very much a problem.

In the Union Officer Survey, leaders were asked the extent to which "skepticism or lack of interest of workers" is a problem. This question was asked to get indirectly at the question of union member commitment as a potential problem affecting the success of joint efforts. Eighty-five percent perceive it to be a problem, with nearly one-third reporting it to be very much a problem.

Chart 5.6

Support for Joint Programs:
Perceptions of Local Union Leaders

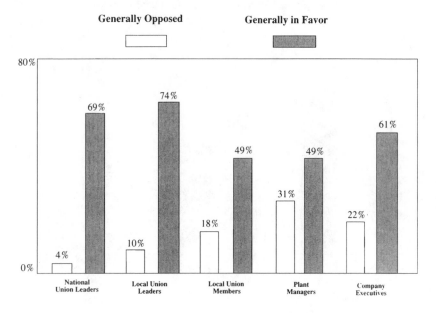

Generally Opposed   Generally in Favor

In an earlier part of the questionnaire to local union leaders, leaders were also asked the following question: "To what extent do the following parties support the establishment of joint labor-management programs?" Chart 5.6 shows the given "parties" and two response categories: generally opposed or generally in favor of joint programs. Not reported in chart 5.6 is the remaining proportion of responses in which a given party is perceived as generally indifferent to joint programs. Note that the responses apply only to those local unions engaged in joint programs.

According to those responses, the party least opposed to joint activities are national union leaders. Here, only 4 percent are perceived to be generally opposed. At the other extreme, 31 percent of the respondents perceive that plant managers are generally opposed to joint programs. In the opposite direction, it is perceived that 69 percent of national union leaders, 74 percent of local union leaders, and 61 percent of company executives are generally in favor of joint programs. However, just under 50 percent of local union members and plant managers are perceived to generally favor joint programs. Overall, based on local union leader perceptions, the least enthusiastic parties to cooperation are local union members and plant-level managers.

Finally, in regard to commitment, in the Headquarters Executive Survey, the top labor relations or human resource executive was asked two questions that indirectly address company headquarters' commitment to cooperative efforts in manufacturing plants. The first was, "In general, company executives are: not in favor of, in favor of, indifferent to joint management-union programs or activities." Restricting the subsample of responses to those headquarters in which at least one plant reported having joint activities, the following responses were obtained: 78 percent generally in favor, 14 percent generally indifferent, and 8 percent generally not in favor of joint activities.

The second related question asked was, "Specifically, the company has: (a) instructed plant management to actively pursue joint management-union activities, (b) instructed management NOT to engage in joint management-union activities, (c) left the decision to engage in joint management-union activities to plant-level managers." The following responses were obtained: 46 percent instructed plant management to pursue cooperation, 50 percent left decisions to plant management, and 4 percent instructed plant management not to pursue joint activities.

As with the problem of perceived distrust, the perceived lack of commitment is a problem that affects the success of a majority of joint programs. As with distrust, lack of commitment (at least its perception) is a serious problem, in one form or another, for one-quarter to one-third of the parties involved in cooperative activities.

Finally, there is bound to be a high association between the problems of trust and commitment. That is, commitment is hard to attain when trust is questioned and a high level of trust is hard to accomplish when commitment from any of the parties is perceived to be problematic. This association is demonstrated, for example, by the high correlations between responses to the Plant Manager Survey on the survey questions pertinent to trust and commitment as problems. The zero order correlations between responses to the question about (a) the extent of sufficient trust between the parties as a problem and responses to the questions about (b) the extent of upper management commitment, plant management commitment, and union leader commitment are all very high and statistically significant (ranging from .33 to .50).

Demoralization From Gains Not Gotten

Over time, the enthusiasm for innovative joint activities is known to wane and under severe market conditions, the intensity of effort appears to decline. In the Union Officer Survey, leaders were asked several questions about the extent to which demoralizing outcomes were problematic for the successful maintenance of joint activities. In the first question, union leaders were asked the extent to which "expected gains from programs not gotten" were a problem. As reported in chart 5.7, approximately 80 percent respond that not attaining expected gains was a problem. Nearly 30 percent report this factor to be very much a problem. Nearly 80 percent of the respondents also find that "insufficient job security" is problematic. Indeed 40 percent report the issue of employment security to be very much a problem.It has also been reported that turnover of key management and union leaders, who have played instrumental roles in spearheading or managing joint activities, has a demoralizing or at least a detrimental effect on program success. In asking union leaders about the extent to which the "turnover of key managers" or "key union leaders" has proven to be problematic, the response indicates that union leaders find turnover of key managers much more problematic than turnover of key union leaders. Just over 60 percent find management turnover as problematic, but less than 30 percent find union leader turnover as problematic. At the extremes, 20

Chart 5.7

Demoralization As a Problem

(Union Leader Response)

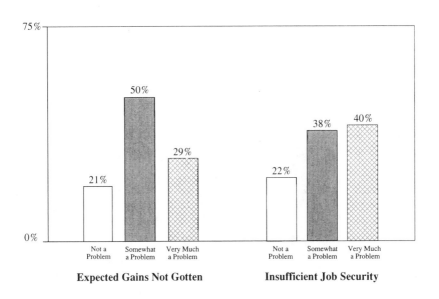

Not a Problem	Somewhat a Problem	Very Much a Problem

Expected Gains Not Gotten   **Insufficient Job Security**

percent find management turnover as very much a problem, whereas only 7 percent find union leader turnover as very much a problem.

Juxtaposing Cooperation and Traditional Collective Bargaining

A fundamental thesis underlying our analysis of cooperation is that the successful implementation, maintenance, and expansion of joint activities require that the parties find ways to juxtapose cooperation and more traditional collective bargaining. In addition to what has been presented in earlier chapters, the parties were directly asked how problematic it is to juxtapose these two dimensions of the relationship.

Chart 5.8

Juxtaposing Cooperation and Contract Negotiations

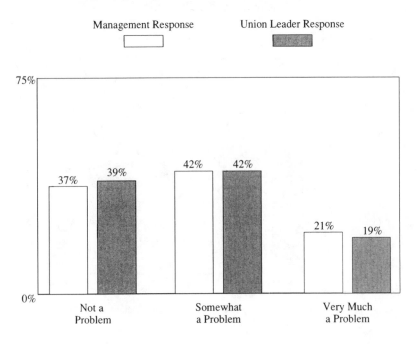

Reported in chart 5.8 and 5.9 are responses to two questions which asked the parties the extent to which they have had difficulty "juxtaposing cooperation" or "balancing joint activities" with contract negotiations and contract administration. As shown in the charts, the majority of managers and union leaders find that juxtaposing joint activities with contract negotiations and administration presents problems. About 20 percent of all respondents report juxtaposing cooperation and contract negotiations as very much a problem. Likewise, about 20 percent of managers find juxtaposing cooperation and day-to-day contract administration very much of a problem, but only 12 percent of union leaders report this to be very much of a problem.

In many respects, the issue of juxtaposing relative power and cooper-

Chart 5.9

Juxtaposing Cooperation and Contract Administration

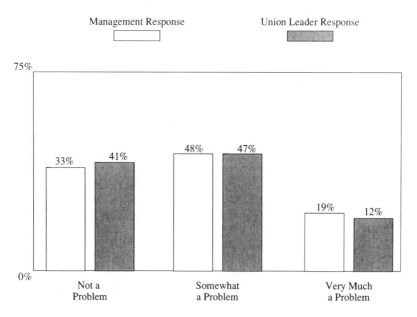

ative power envelops the problematic issues of distrust, perceived lack of commitment, and demoralization from gains not gotten. The exercise or threat of using relative power depicts a process in which distrust is magnified as traditional conflicts are rekindled and old wounds are opened. Commitment to cooperation is likewise challenged when either party uses relative power advantages to maximize its overall gains. Often enough, cooperative activities are held "hostage," i.e., put on hold until adversarial conflicts are satisfactorily resolved. Demoralization with cooperation is also often heightened. In this latter regard, resolution of conflicts of interest via relative power raises the important concern over fair and equitable distribution of overall gains (or losses). The difficult process of identifying and distributing gains derived directly or indirectly from cooperative activities is visited or revisited.

All this does not imply that hard bargaining and legalistic contract administration necessarily undermine cooperation. Indeed, what is learned from cooperation with respect to joint problemsolving often improves the negotiation and contract administration process. The potential for diminishing the cooperative process, however, must be recognized and dealt with effectively if cooperation is not to be diminished or destroyed. This is not to suggest, however, that the parties should resort to short-sighted compromising in the spirit of demonstrating commitment to cooperative relations. Several prescriptions designed to help labor and management avoid serious problems and minimize unwanted and unnecessary consequences are proposed in chapter 6.

6

Implications and Prescriptions for Making Partnerships Work

In this final chapter, I first briefly discuss several fundamental implications derived from the analyses presented in the first five chapters. Second, I propose several fairly general prescriptions that may hold some promise of enhancing labor-management partnerships — for those parties, of course, choosing to cooperate. In this chapter I take the liberty of releasing myself from the burden of providing empirical documentation or support for either the implications drawn or prescriptions proposed. My intention here is to open a debate and discussion, not test the soundness of any propositions.

Implications

One overriding implication of the present inquiry is that neither labor nor management can avoid making some hard choices fundamental to their relationships. It appears that for most American unions and companies, the choices faced are either all-out conflict or all-out cooperation. The traditional ways simply don't work well in highly competitive and volatile markets. Indeed, there is no option of maintaining or returning to the "good old days" of traditional collective bargaining.

In thinking about alternative labor-relations strategies, it seems reasonable to assume that some companies have selected and designed strategies to deunionize; and they have done so without any or with very little consideration of choosing cooperation. In these companies, unions face no choice. They are forced to challenge the company. Weaker unions will simply lose, but strong unions have some opportunity to force a shift in management strategies. Failing to seek or failing to force a shift to cooperation, strong unions will slowly destroy the companies and themselves in battle. Needless to say, this scenario will prove to be a hollow victory for all parties concerned. But for recalcitrant employers unwilling to cooperate, strong unions cannot sit back and watch their own institutions destroyed while these employers are allowed to have their aggressive way unopposed.

Alternatively, some companies seek to cooperate initially but their union leader counterparts cannot find their way to cooperate. Denied by their unions the choice of cooperation, these companies are forced (and perhaps easily so) to embark on union avoidance strategies—companywide or in given plants where local unions refuse to cooperate. Again, weak unions will lose and unnecessarily so. Strong unions will lose in the longer run, unless they recognize that traditional adversarial relations won't work and they too eventually embrace cooperation. One can imagine, however, that the longer unions deny management the choice of cooperation, the less likely management will be interested in shifting course, especially where management has reduced union strength over time via union avoidance and deunionization strategies.

The general implication, therefore, is that, except in that handful of unionized settings not seriously threatened by domestic or global competitors, unions have little choice but to cooperate. A second implication, on the other hand, is that unions have many choices regarding what cooperation looks like. In making these choices, the focus is on the *means* of cooperation not the fundamental goals of unions or management. The union still seeks to gain as much as possible for its membership in compensation and in the terms and conditions of employment. Management still seeks to optimize profits. In general terms, therefore, cooperation does not require (indeed, it cannot require) the parties to shift their fundamental priority goals, or the fundamental values and ideologies underlying these goals. Instead, cooperation requires that the parties shift their values and ideologies about the *means* of pursuing priority goals. The prescriptions proposed in the next section address some of the more important shifts along this line.

A third implication is that relative power plays an important check-and-balance role in cooperative efforts. Choosing to cooperate does not change the inherent conflict of interests between management and union. The wealth generated from the employment context will always require dividing and relative power will always underlie any mechanism for dividing it. Consequently, as in any traditional collective bargaining relationship, attention to the relative power of one's own organization is essential. This implication, given changes in the market, is perhaps most important to unions. Diminished relative power not only undermines a union's ability to maximize gain via the process of dividing wealth, but also undermines the cooperative effort to increase the wealth to be divided. This implication is consistent with the empirical analyses of performance and labor relations outcomes presented in chapter 4 and the problems examined in chapter 5.

A fourth implication is that in highly competitive markets, "everything else the same," employers cannot endure incurring higher costs per unit of labor input. Unions, however, must obtain some combination of higher levels of compensation and better workplace environments than is obtained by employees of nonunion competitors, else employees have insufficient reason to retain or select union representation. It is imperative to union survival, therefore, that not "everything else be the same." Unions must offer some added value to production that offsets any differential in compensation and workplace environment costs.

Cooperation offers that potential added value, given that union leaders provide an effective voice mechanism that leads to improved quality, greater efficiencies, productivity, or other cost reductions. Such a perspective assumes that the workforce and union leadership are well equipped to devise ways of organizing work and work relationships effectively. One might argue, however, that the same gains can be accomplished in nonunion settings and, hence, unions cannot provide sufficient added value relative to their nonunion competitors. That alternative argument holds if management in nonunion settings provides equivalent mechanisms for employee input and effectively utilizes that input. My limited observation indicates that a large majority of American managers do not willingly or purposely share their decisionmaking authority and status with their workforces. Without constraints imposed, managers who are less open to seeking the input of employees and sharing authority with them act in ways that do not maximize efficiencies and productivity.

Here, union leaders with the support of their members can constrain reluctant managers, insisting upon the sharing of decisionmaking and responsibility. By being worthy advocates of effective employee input, union leaders have before them a mechanism upon which to obtain higher compensation and better workplace environments for their memberships and at the same time provide the added value to the enterprise to offset these added labor costs. Effective advocacy, however, demands that union leaders be far better equipped or skilled in the business functions of finance, operations, marketing, and human resource management. This does not imply that they become businessmen and businesswomen. It implies that they understand the market and organizational constraints of running a competitive enterprise, that they become the experts of human resource management, and that they, in turn, act vigorously as the advocates of the workforce. As advocates of the workforce (which notably requires no change in union philosophy), union leaders view the workforce as the key set of stakeholders in the enterprise. As such, their role is to construct and pursue avenues that effectively elevate the importance of legitimate workforce interests as stakeholders of the enterprise. In doing so, union leaders must be able to demonstrate that satisfying important interests of the workforce leads to added value, at least equivalent to the added costs of satisfying the interests of the workforce. As discussed subsequently, the interests of employees as stakeholders will need to be balanced with the interests of other stakeholders of the enterprise.

Finally, a central implication of the present analysis is that it is imperative the parties find ways to sufficiently mitigate the salient problems that undermine successful cooperation. Unless these problems can be dealt with effectively, the long-run prospects that cooperative efforts will have handsome payoffs are greatly limited.

Prescriptions for Long-Term Successful Cooperation

In this section, several prescriptions are proposed that are designed to avoid, mitigate, or resolve problems that undermine successful cooperation. They are proposed in a spirit that recognizes that in each labor-management setting, the relationship is unique, unique in history, with unique personalities, and with unique organizational and market constraints. The given parties, therefore, are best equipped to establish detailed mechanisms or processes around each prescription that follows.

Establish Triggers and Procedures for Resolving Serious Problems and Crises

The evidence indicates that a majority of efforts wane after a short period of time, and history shows that some efforts collapse (without much forewarning) under the weight of market pressures or flagrant violations of trust and commitment. It is proposed herein that the parties establish some trigger mechanism and a process to resolve disputes over problems or events that seriously threaten the livelihood of cooperative efforts.

Such a trigger mechanism and process, of course, have already been developed for resolving disputes over rights embodied in contracts. Because the parties cannot foresee all the problems and disputes that undoubtedly will arise during the term of negotiated contracts, grievance procedures (usually with outside arbitration as a final step) have been implemented. The parties are allowed to grieve when problems arise, and grievance procedures provide an acceptable due process mechanism for resolution of disputes. In turn, grievance procedures provide a means for accomplishing labor-management stability; they are essentially a *quid pro quo* for eliminating strike threats, strikes, and other workplace disruptions during the life of agreements.

The strategic shift to joint activities is also wrought with unknown events and reactions that can undermine cooperative efforts—much like problems that test the rights and responsibilities negotiated in contracts. It is proposed, therefore, that a parallel structure or mechanism designed to resolve disputes associated with cooperative activities be created. Here I would highly recommend that when a majority of the joint steering or policy committee believe the cooperative effort is seriously threatened, that a trusted (and preselected) mediator or neutral consultant be called in to help resolve disputes. Such a trigger (i.e., the vote of the committee) allows the parties to begin constructively tackling the problem at hand, instead of allowing it to have unintended and unnecessary negative snowballing effects.

This proposed mechanism would allow both management and the union leadership to explain to all parties that a serious problem (or problems) has been recognized and that the issue is being dealt with constructively and jointly through the mediation process, which was jointly decided beforehand. Once a resolution has been reached jointly, the resolution would be jointly presented to all the parties. This kind of procedure not only allows the parties to more effectively construct a resolution, it also is intended to help insure that cooperative activities remain intensive instead of dwindling, being held hostage, or at the extreme destroyed (à la Eastern Airlines).

Negotiate Trust and Commitment

One theme that is heard over and over (albeit not in every setting) is that "you can't trust em" and "they're really not committed" to this effort. Cooperation is a highly demanding exercise and it is clear that behaviors that increase distrust between parties and/or imply that either party is not sufficiently committed to the cooperative effort undermine it. It is important to recognize that assessments of trust and commitment are based on perceptions, some accurate and some not. In order to reduce the occurrence and magnitude of the effects of perceived violations of trust and commitment, the second proposal prescribes that the parties negotiate definitions and expectations of trust and commitment. By "negotiate" I do not mean to imply contractually binding rights. The overall objective is to delineate the kind of behaviors that lead each party to infer that the other party has violated or diminished the level of trust or commitment and to reach a compromise that both parties agree to live by.

By negotiating trust and commitment, each party has an opportunity to explain its view of what is expected from the other party. For instance, consider the following true but anonymous case. Division headquarters informed plant management that they intended to subcontract out a small proportion of plant production, which would displace 10 to 12 hourly employees. Affected employees were informed of their anticipated displacement. After consultation with the local union chairman, an alternative proposal was devised at the plant and, in turn, accepted by division-level management. The affected employees were then notified by both the plant superintendent and local chairman that a solution had been found and they would not be displaced. A few days later, however, the plant superintendent was notified that division management had reversed its decision. The superintendent (without further consultation with the local chairman) informed the employees that the subcontracting decision had been reversed. In the eyes of the union membership, its leadership in this case appeared to have no control over or input into such key decisions; worse yet, the leadership appeared to have been coopted by management. Having lost faith in the cooperative process and support from its membership, the local union leadership sent out the word to the rank-and-file that management was not to be trusted and that the leadership now had serious reservations about ongoing joint activities.

By discussing the kind of behaviors that diminish or violate trust and the kind of responses that can be expected from such violations, the parties can then negotiate behaviors that enhance cooperation, not undermine it. In the above example, one condition of trust that could have been negotiated is that any announcement or notification concerning displacement from subcontracting must first be presented to the union leadership or, going further, announced jointly. In addition, the parties could have agreed that the union leadership is not to withdraw its support for joint activities until a given perceived violation of trust is fully investigated and discussed within the appropriate joint steering or policy committee.

Negotiation over an acceptable definition and acceptable behaviors with respect to expected commitment to cooperative efforts is likewise proposed. For example, take the case where a supervisor has decided to have employees regularly work overtime instead of recalling laid-off union members. To the local union leader, this may be perceived as a violation of commitment to cooperation if, indeed, the union leader wants laid-off members recalled. As a form of political retaliation, the union leader encourages members not to volunteer for team-based activities the supervisor wants.

Upon discussion and negotiation, a solution to the above incident may become clear. In the present actual case, the supervisor assumed he was doing the right thing for the union; he had polled his employees, who overwhelmingly voted to work overtime instead of recalling laid-off members. However, the supervisor never queried the union leader for his preferences. Angered, the union leader failed to discuss in any detail with the supervisor, the dispute between them. Had the parties defined and negotiated acceptable behaviors as they pertain to expectations about commitment, the problematic circumstances that effectively led to withdrawal of support for cooperation by the union leader could have been avoided. Here, one could imagine that agreement could have been reached in advance that supervision and the union leadership were obligated to jointly decide the issue of overtime vs. recall anytime the extent of overtime exceeded an agreed upon level. More broadly, the parties could agree that supervision is not to make assumptions about union leader preferences. It could also have been agreed that the union leadership is obligated to consult with supervision when normal supervisory discretion is perceived as being inconsistent with expectations of commitment.

As part of negotiating trust and commitment, the parties will need to establish a means or procedure by which to settle disputes and repair relations over violations of agreed upon behaviors. Those behaviors that lead to serious disruption perhaps can be best resolved using the procedures developed under the first proposal above. Less serious infractions can be addressed and resolved by members of an appropriate joint steering or policy committee. As a first step, the manager or union representative who perceives that a representative of the union or management has violated trust and/or commitment (as it has been negotiated) is obligated to bring it immediately to the attention of that individual. If after private conversation about the perceived violation, the individuals to the dispute cannot resolve it in a mutually satisfactory way, then other members (if not all members) of the joint steering committee are invited to discuss the dispute and help formulate a resolution. The key here is that a procedure requiring immediate attention to problems of trust and commitment be established, that the parties know well in advance that certain actions or behaviors will be immediately challenged, and that both labor and management are part of an agreeable resolution.

Finally, perceptions are often inaccurate. In sensitive labor-management interactions, misperceptions are often the case, especially as the parties move from strictly adversarial relations to cooperative arrangements. In the example above of perceived violation of commitment, the supervisor was genuinely surprised at the union officer's reaction to the use of overtime. By negotiating expectations of sufficient trust and commitment and by immediately bringing any perceptions of violations of trust and commitment to the attention of presumed offenders, many misperceptions would be cleared up and truly unnecessary withdrawal avoided.

Establish Labor's Claim to Stake in Business Decisions and Performance Gains

As first presented in the theoretical discussion in chapter 2, cooperation requires a different perspective and approach to labor's input into management decisions and the division of gains than is required by traditional collective bargaining. In traditional collective bargaining, the division of gains is primarily determined by the relative power of the parties. The introduction of cooperation, however, carries with it an expectation that gains are shared fairly, according to each party's contribution to that gain. The clash inherent upon introducing cooperation to a traditional adversarial relationship clearly demands that the parties

- identify where and how much union input into company decisions is expected;

- agree to how union input contributes to cooperative gains (directly and indirectly); and

- agree to the union's share of income and security rewards derivable from cooperation.

Where and How Much Input

In order to distribute fairly the gains derived from cooperation, it is essential that the parties first agree as to where cooperative input is expected. The organizational arrangements for union leader and member input is wide-ranging. These arrangements include employee ownership and control (e.g. Weirton Steel and the Independent Steelworkers Union), consensus decisionmaking from top-to-bottom (UAW and GM, Saturn Corporation), membership on company boards of directors (e.g., currently, Chrysler and the UAW, and at one time Eastern Airlines and the Machinists), and more traditional structures with extensive cooperative activities but with ultimate executive authority (e.g., Xerox and the Amalgamated Clothing and Textile Workers Union, and Ford and the UAW).

It is clear in any case that the choices for organizational arrangements for union leader and member input are wide-ranging. One would search in vain to find a satisfactory theoretical or empirical justification for considering any one form as optimal across all settings. But, pragmatically, the parties can only benefit in the long run if they can fashion an agreeable organizational arrangement regarding the points of union input and the extent of that input. Problems enveloping trust and commitment arise from the lack of clarity or agreement as to the appropriate degree of input and the points at which union input is expected. For instance, it is heard frequently enough that plant-level joint decisions are unilaterally overridden or "put on the back burner" by managers or executives at the division or corporate level. These experiences can only seriously frustrate the efforts at the plant level by undermining expectations of company commitment to cooperation, unless, of course, it has been agreed upon by both labor and management that joint decisionmaking occurs only at the plant level. If both parties or the union at the plant level conclude that it is essential to the success of plant-level cooperation to have division- or corporate-level joint decisionmaking, then arrangements need to be made to provide for upper-level union input into upper-level management decisions.

The form and degree of union input or participation within the hierarchy of the company must also be determined. For some union leaders and/or their management counterparts, the acceptable choice is that the top union leadership be consulted prior to company decisions. For others, the choice may be some degree of union membership on boards of directors, or regular consultation with executive committees, or some form of majority or consensus decisionmaking by upper-level joint policy committees. For others, the agreeable choice may be that union input and participation be restricted to within the scope of traditional plant-level decisions.

Although some observers of cooperative activities may argue that union input at all levels of the company structure is essential to the overall success of cooperative efforts, the real key is that the parties have identified and sufficiently clarified the various points and degree of union input and have agreed that these arrangements satisfy each party's interests. The primary objective here is to eliminate misperceptions by either labor or management as to where and how much input the union is to have into traditional management decisions. Misperceptions of this kind lead to serious problems of trust and commitment and, furthermore, they make it very difficult to ascertain labor's claim to cooperative gains.

Determine How Union Input Contributes to Performance Gains

Having established and clarified where and how much union input is expected, the parties must next identify how union input contributes to overall company performance. Centrally important to an equitable distribution or sharing of gains from cooperation is the clarification of that portion of any recognizable gain that is attributable to cooperative activities. By way of example, if the company makes sizable capital investments that lead to productivity gains, are these considered gains obtained outside the cooperative effort? If efficiency gains are obtained through elimination of restrictive work practices via concession bargaining, are these gains treated as coming from outside cooperative efforts? If overall company performance improves (or worsens) due to the performance of nonproduction business units or nonbargaining units (e.g., from financial arms of the company), are these gains or losses considered outside cooperative efforts?

Acceptable answers to these questions obviously must be decided by the parties themselves. In some settings, the input of the union at the corporate level may have led management to make capital investments they otherwise would have foregone. Or capital investment decisions may have been borne directly from proposals generated by joint team-based efforts at a given facility. Or in other instances, employers may have based their investment decisions in part on the fact that joint activities at the plant would maximize the returns to such investments. As in the above examples where capital investment decisions are shaped directly or indirectly by union involvement, unions typically will have expectations that gains so derived are to be shared equitably. In other settings or instances, management decisions on capital investments may have been made independently of any union input or weight given to more cooperative relations or joint programs at the plant level. Perceived as such, managers will expect any gains tied to capital investment as theirs, except to the extent that labor via its relative power can demand some of the gain.

With respect to gains obtained from concession bargaining, one could imagine that in some cases unions agreed to the elimination of restrictive practices as a *quid pro quo* for greater union input and participation in traditional management decisions. As a *quid pro quo*, the union leadership and its members may very well expect to share the gains from concessions, since they would not otherwise have agreed to them. In other cases, efficiencies derived from concessions could not have occurred without a much more trustful relationship having been developed through earlier cooperative efforts. As such, union leaders and members may perceive they are entitled to share these indirect cooperative gains. In the third example above, management may hold that any profitability derived from production or nonproduction business units in which no cooperative efforts are ongoing is not subject to sharing, except as bargained for. Unions may hold otherwise, believing that these other units indirectly profit from business units in which cooperation does take place. By way of example, if a company's financial arm that provides credit to customers is profitable, the union may perceive that its profitability is tied to the priçe and quality of products sold. Because price and quality have been made more attractive by cooperative efforts in producing that product, the union can argue that the business unit providing attractive financing has benefited in part and indirectly from cooperation. Hence some of the profitability derived from the company's financial credit arm is expected to be shared, without resort to adversarial negotiations.

The level of aggregation to which cooperative gains are tied is also a key issue to be decided. Is the profitability to be shared tied only to a given plant's performance, or to its division or operating company's performance, or to overall corporate performance? When either party believes any cooperative gains to be shared are based on a different level of profit aggregation than the other party so perceives, then the parties will remain in dispute over how the pie is to be shared — simply because the potential size of the pie has not been agreed upon. Again, expectations of receiving equitable sharing of cooperative gains are thwarted and problems of perceived distrust and lack of commitment go unresolved.

Agree On Equitable Sharing of Cooperative Gains

Finally, having agreed upon where in the organization there is to be cooperative input, the extent of that input, and how that input contributes directly and indirectly to cooperative gains, the parties need to resolve differences of opinion regarding equitable sharing. As discussed, although each party always prefers more over less, each party ultimately wants nothing less than their perceived contribution to any gain generated by cooperative activities. As one can readily imagine, determining an equitable share becomes exceedingly complex. First, it is difficult enough to accurately measure overall improvements, be they productivity, quality, or efficiency gains. Except in the simplest contexts, accurately measuring any gains due in full or in part to cooperation is probably impossible. For example, how does one measure labor's contribution to cooperative gains derived from upper-level management consultation with upper-level union leadership? How does one measure labor's contribution to gains derived from capital investments, either with respect to labor's input into those decisions or labor's utilization of capital investments?

Second, not all performance gains or losses are due to cooperative efforts. Yet the parties must reach some agreement as to what portion of performance gains, if any, are to be divided based on equitable sharing, the remaining portion to be divided by traditional bargaining. In spite of the difficulty, if not impossibility, of accurately measuring the portion of any overall gain attributable to cooperation and then measuring each party's contribution to those cooperative gains, the parties still must reach an explicit agreement of sharing the fruits of cooperation.

From the union's viewpoint, sharing the fruits of cooperation has as much to do with job security as it does with compensation. The demoralization that arises from continued employment losses cannot be underestimated. Hence, agreements on sharing performance gains must be fashioned around compensation and employment security.

With respect to compensation, some negotiated formula for performance gain sharing—be it gainsharing, profit sharing, and/or stock ownership—should be negotiated. The formulas are used to make explicit labor and management's equitable shares of performance improvements. As best the parties can, these performance sharing plans should be tied to the various levels or points of cooperative input throughout the organization.

At the plant level in multiplant companies, gainsharing based on productivity or performance benchmarks may be most appropriate in sharing gains (if any) from cooperative input at that level of organizations. The formulas established necessarily should reflect the agreed upon intensity or degree of input from labor. That is, formulas used should satisfactorily reflect the perceptions of the amount of input for each kind of input (i.e., the points of input) by labor and management. For instance, if capital investments are made, the parties must agree how much, if any, performance improvements derived from capital investments go to labor. Where management decides and acts unilaterally to make capital investments, but those decisions are predicated on the union's cooperative spirit, then the negotiated formula should reflect some measure of sharing any gains with labor as derived from such investments. One can imagine that the union's proportionate share would be smaller (say 10 percent of gains) than where capital investment decisions were first proposed by joint teams or joint committees. Here, the parties may agree that 25 or 50 percent of gains are to be shared with labor. Similarly, the parties must address the proportion of gains to be shared as derived from all other forms of union input and participation at the plant. The key, of course, is tying the proportion of gains to the degree of union input that leads to performance improvements.

As we move up the organization hierarchy to the division, group, or operating company level and then on to corporate headquarters, measuring cooperative input and gains from cooperation becomes even more complex (and in many cases, perhaps hopelessly so). Some performance-sharing formula, however, must still be devised. Again, the parties must decide the form of sharing and base that sharing on the points of cooperative input. Given the added complexity and the more steps removed from the cooperative input, it would be advisable that the parties fashion some sort of profit sharing and/or stock ownership plan. Although more removed from the actual cooperative input, the ambiguity inherent in tracing cooperative input to cooperative output demands a more ambiguous performance-sharing formula. It remains essential though that both labor and management come to agree that the method and formula used reflect the parties' joint effort to tie performance gains, at least roughly so, to cooperative gains (gotten both directly and indirectly).

In summary, by constructing acceptable performance gain formulas, the parties make explicit their perceptions and expectations of equitable sharing from cooperative efforts and they distinguish between gains (or losses) derived from traditional collective bargaining and those derived from cooperation. In so doing, the parties eliminate (or greatly minimize) misperceptions about labor's claim to the company's wealth.

Performance sharing arrangements also carry with them other advantages. First they provide a mechanism by which the parties can better assess and monitor their performance. As discussed in chapter 4, it appears that performance gains from cooperation peak after a few years and then decline. By better monitoring of successes and failures, if and when performance begins to decline, the parties can more quickly and vigorously tackle the factors or problems leading to waning performance. Second, advocates of performance-sharing arrangements largely premise their advocation on the grounds that such plans provide financial incentive for employees to become more committed to attaining performance improvements. As such, employees are more inclined to actively participate in joint activities and more aggressively seek solutions to problems and barriers impeding performance. Finally, it is generally argued that performance-sharing arrangements not only allow employees to share in the responsibility and gains of improving company performance but also to share the risks associated with running a business. By sharing the rewards and risks, employees are expected to become more in tune with good business practices and managers are expected to become more in tune with good employee and labor-management relations practices. In turn, both parties learn to engage in more optimal employment-related behaviors.

As recognized above, compensation is only part of the performance-sharing equation; employment security is another. Underlying cooperation is the important notion that each party learns to better appreciate the special interests of the other party. Underlying the trust and commitment surrounding cooperation is the important notion that each party (having recognized and having a better understanding of the legitimate interests of the other) becomes more committed to seeing those legitimate interests obtained. The issue at hand and one central to the long-run success of cooperative efforts is employment security. Along these lines, employees and union representatives expect that operational decisions give considerable weight to potential employment displacement. Several examples may best illustrate this point.

Strategic operational decisions about the opening and location of new facilities, the assignment of new product lines, the closing or idling of facilities, subcontracting bargaining unit work, and capital investments have been (short of contractual and NLRB-imposed restrictions) the exclusive domain of management decisionmaking. In cooperative settings, however, the potential for substantial displacement carries with it an expectation by labor that (1) management will seek alternative business plans that minimize displacement while satisfying other legitimate business concerns, and (2) those local parties who have worked the hardest at cooperation will be the least adversely affected. These legitimate expectations by unions require that strategic operational decisions be influenced by employment security concerns. They obligate management, furthermore, to reward local parties who have demonstrated their commitment to making joint activities successful. It is proposed herein that labor and management negotiate or management make explicit up front (a) the factors that are weighed in making various strategic operational decisions, (b) the weight or ranking among factors of the importance given to displacement of employees, and (c) the weight or ranking among factors given to the success of local joint efforts in improving productivity, quality, and operational efficiencies.

This proposal is not to imply that employment security or the rewarding of local cooperative efforts are factors to be given the top priority among all other factors (albeit that may be the optimal solution in some cases). Instead, the above proposal requires the parties to agree over the weighting or ranking among other factors of employment security and rewarding local parties for their cooperative efforts. Having reached an acceptable agreement, the parties are agreeing (at least for the present and until renegotiated) that they can live by the agreement, without misperceptions that lead to rising mistrust and diminishing commitment to cooperation.

Summary and Conclusions
New Partnerships or Going in Circles?

Because of enormous and unrelenting market forces at work, labor-management relations have had to change. The volatility of the market during the late 1970s and throughout most of the 1980s, coupled with long-run market pressures, have required that unionized organizations become far more adaptable and flexible and that they continually improve performance. At the corporate level of highly unionized manufacturing, three grand labor relations strategies are currently being pursued: Union-Avoidance, Cooperation, and a Mixed strategy encompassing elements of both union-avoidance and cooperation. In the short run, Cooperators appear to have gained the edge with respect to improving corporate performance. The longer-run outcome regarding which strategy may prevail, however, is still in the making.

Primarily influenced by the strategic choices of their parent headquarters, roughly half of the unionized manufacturing plants in the U.S. have embarked on formalized cooperative activities. These activities include joint team-based and committee-based programs. Only the more intensive joint programs in these plants appear to be having positive effects on plant performance and on labor-management relationships. Where there are secure unions and high degrees of union leader participation, gains are all the more sizable. Where employment continues to decline and employers engage in subcontracting out bargaining unit work, gains from cooperation are difficult to achieve. The evidence also indicates that the positive returns to joint efforts typically wane after a few years.

Several general types of problems are typically encountered in cooperative settings, problems that can seriously undermine the cooperative spirit. These problems include violations of or insufficient trust and commitment, demoralization from employment insecurity and anticipated gains not achieved, and the inherent difficulties of juxtaposing or interweaving traditional collective bargaining and cooperation.

Based on empirical analyses reported herein, several general implications for unions can be derived. First, in the great majority of cases, unions have little choice but to cooperate, because even traditional adversarial relations of the past are no longer available to them. Second, however, unions have many choices to make about what cooperation entails. Third, union leaders, as advocates for the general welfare and benefit of employees, must become tomorrow's human resource management experts and must understand far better the running of a profitable business. As advocates and experts, union leaders have the opportunity to improve the lives of their members and simultaneously show management the full potential for deriving necessary added value via the improved management and utilization of its human resources.

American history shows that cooperation has been a short-lived experience for nearly all unionized organizations. The widespread "experimentation" of the present era, however, is unusual and signals that conditions have greatly changed, giving some indication that cooperation in U.S. industry may ultimately become a workable alternative. Nevertheless, the parties must find ways to avoid the pitfalls that have destroyed earlier cooperative efforts. It is in this spirit that several prescriptions for long-term success are proposed: namely, establish triggers and procedures to resolve serious problems and crises, negotiate trust and commitment, and establish and clarify labor's stake in business decisionmaking and labor's claim to sharing performance gains.

Competitive threats to unionized enterprises have spurred cooperation, but those competitive threats can also destroy cooperative efforts by pitting proponents and opponents of cooperation (within both management and union ranks) against one another, as organizations faced by shrinking markets struggle to find a way out. In that struggle, many parties may lose by simply going in circles, with the potential fruits of cooperation only an illusion. Those who can form workable partnerships, on the other hand, with their eyes focused on continuous improvement in their relations, are very likely to be tomorrow's winners.

Appendix A

PLANT MANAGER SURVEY
Survey of Plants: Management-Union Cooperation Research Project

Management-union cooperative programs as defined for present purposes refer to activities devised and/or undertaken jointly with unions. The focus of such programs may be on company performance (for example, productivity committees or quality control circles), and/or worker satisfaction and well being (for example, quality of work life, employee involvement, and safety and health). Activities may also entail some form of incentive arrangement to increase company profitability and employee compensation (for example, Scanlon or Rucker gainsharing plans and profit sharing or ESOPs that include activities designed to increase employee involvement).

If you have *never* established any such joint programs, please complete sections I, II, III and VII. If you *have* established any such program, even if it has not been fully implemented or has been terminated, please complete all sections of this questionnaire.

Section I. Program Identification

Below is a table that identifies several kinds of programs. Under the various stages of the process identified at the top of the table, please provide the approximate month and year for each of the applicable stages.

Even if you have **not** established any kind of joint program, please indicate under column 1 if the establishment of **any kind of joint** programs was given serious initial consideration, and if so, when.

157

Program/Activity	Considered but Decided Against		Oversight or Steering Committee Established		Program Activities Began		Program Activity Became Widespread		Program Terminated		NOT a Joint Program
	Month	Year	Month	Year	Month	Year	Month	Year	Month	Year	
1. Quality of Work Life											
2. Productivity Committee											
3. Quality Control Circles											
4. Work Teams											
5. Training Committee											
6. Industrial Relations Com. (general problem solving)											
7. Scanlon Plan											
8. Rucker Plan											
9. Other Gainsharing Plan											
10. Health and Safety Comm.											
11. Substance Abuse Comm.											
12. ESOP (with employee involvement activities)											
13. Profit Sharing (with employee involvement activities)											
14. Other (describe)											

Even if you have established or terminated any of the programs identified below and they are **not jointly coordinated efforts with the union**, please check this in the last column.

Section II. General Information About Plant

1. What proportion of production workers are under the union contract identified in the cover letter? _____ %

2. How many unions represent employees in your plant? _____

3. What proportion of non-exempt office employees are under a union contract? _____ %

4. What is the average length of employment within the bargaining unit? _____ years

5. What proportion of the bargaining unit employees are female? _____ %

6. Since 1975, what has been the extent of capital expenditures on new technologies or automation within the plant?

   Substantial _____ Modest _____ None _____ $_____

7. Since 1975, what proportion of the bargaining unit employees have lost their jobs in the plant because of the introduction of new technologies or automation? _____ %

8. Since 1975, what proportion of bargaining unit jobs have been subcontracted out on a permanent basis?

   Substantial _____ Modest _____ None _____ _____ %

9. Since 1975, would you characterize any round of negotiations as "concession" bargaining (i.e., wage or benefit freezes or cut backs, elimination of restrictive work rules, etc)?

   No _____ Yes _____

   If **yes**, in what year or years were such concessions negotiated? _____ _____ _____

10. Is there an Area-Wide Joint Labor-Management Committee in the

locality of your plant?

Yes _____ No _____ Don't know _____

11. Is there an Industry-Wide Joint Labor Management Committee in your industry?

Yes _____ No _____ Don't know _____

Section III. Comparison of 1976-1980 Period to 1981-1985 Period

Comparing the 1976-1980 period to the 1981-1985 period, please indicate the extent to which the variables identified below have changed since the 1976-1980 period.

	Extent of Change				
Variable	Much Higher	Modestly Higher	About the Same	Modestly Lower	Much Lower
1. Total level of production	_____	_____	_____	_____	_____
2. Plant capacity utilization	_____	_____	_____	_____	_____
3. Productivity per unit of labor	_____	_____	_____	_____	_____
4. Product quality	_____	_____	_____	_____	_____
5. Rate of scrappage or waste	_____	_____	_____	_____	_____
6. Restrictiveness of work rules	_____	_____	_____	_____	_____
7. Rate of grievances	_____	_____	_____	_____	_____
8. Rate of absenteeism/tardiness	_____	_____	_____	_____	_____
9. Adversarial relationship with union	_____	_____	_____	_____	_____
10. Adversarial relationship between supervisors and work-force	_____	_____	_____	_____	_____

Section IV. Structure and Focus of Program Activities

A. Including any joint program that may have been terminated, please briefly describe the focus and structure of the joint effort that you consider to be the **most important to management objectives**, excluding health and safety activities. (If you have some documentation describing the focus and structure of this program, feel free to submit that in place of your description under 2 below.)

1. Key problem(s) that led to and is addressed by program: (e.g., productivity, quality, absenteeism)

2. Structure of kind of activities: (e.g., work team arrangements, ad hoc tasks groups, regular meetings for employee input, etc.)

B. In reference to the program identified above, please indicate:

1. the proportion of bargaining unit employees covered by the program: _____ %

2. the frequency of scheduled meetings for

  (a) the highest level steering committee: every _____ weeks

  (b) the lowest level work groups or teams, (if applicable): every _____ weeks

3. the number and proportion of union representatives on the highest level steering committee: # _____   % _____

4. who initially promoted the development of the program:

parent company _____   plant management _____

division headquarters_____   union _____

C. If the program identified above has been terminated, please identify what you believe to be the key factors leading to its termination.

_____

_____

_____

_____

D. To what extent has your plant worked with the following organizations in designing and/or implementing cooperative programs?

Organization	Not at all	Some	Very Much
Area-Wide Joint Labor-Management Committee	____	____	____
Industry-Wide Joint Labor-Management Committee	____	____	____
Federal Mediation and Conciliation Service (FMCS)	____	____	____
U.S. Department of Labor	____	____	____

Section V: Comparison of Conditions Before and After Joint Program Implementation

Comparing the five year period prior to implementation of the most important joint program identified above, please indicate the degree to which the variables identified below have changed.

Extent of Change

Variable	Much Higher	Modestly Higher	About the Same	Modestly Lower	Much Lower
1. Total level of production	_____	_____	_____	_____	_____
2. Plant capacity utilization	_____	_____	_____	_____	_____
3. Productivity per unit of labor	_____	_____	_____	_____	_____
4. Product quality	_____	_____	_____	_____	_____
5. Rate of scrappage or waste	_____	_____	_____	_____	_____
6. Restrictiveness of work rules	_____	_____	_____	_____	_____
7. Rate of grievances	_____	_____	_____	_____	_____
8. Rate of absenteeism/tardiness	_____	_____	_____	_____	_____
9. Adversarial relationship with union	_____	_____	_____	_____	_____
10. Adversarial relationship between supervisors and workforce	_____	_____	_____	_____	_____
11. Cooperative spirit in contract negotiations	_____	_____	_____	_____	_____
12. Other conditions that have changed (describe)					
_____	_____	_____	_____	_____	_____
_____	_____	_____	_____	_____	_____

Section VI. Difficulties in Implementing and Maintaining Joint Program Activities

Problems obviously arise as joint program activities are implemented. To what extent have the following problems affected the successful implementation and maintenance of your most important joint program, identified above?

Extent of Problem

Potential Problems	Not a Problem	Somewhat a Problem	Very much a Problem	Important Factor in Termination of Program
1. Lack of experience or expertise in devising and implementing joint programs.	___	___	___	___
2. Lack of sufficient trust between parties.	___	___	___	___
3. Lack of adequate preparation of plant management for change.	___	___	___	___
4. Lack of adequate orientation and training for bargaining unit employees.	___	___	___	___
5. Perceived lack of commitment by upper management.	___	___	___	___
6. Lack of broad commitment among plant managers.	___	___	___	___
7. Lack of broad commitment by union leaders.	___	___	___	___
8. Difficulty juxtaposing cooperation and contract negotiations.	___	___	___	___
9. Difficulty juxtaposing cooperation and contract administration.	___	___	___	___

Other that the potential problems identified above, please briefly describe other problems that you have encountered and/or elaborate, if you wish, on any of potential problems identified above.

_____

_____

_____

_____

Section VII.

Please identify the top labor relations executive at the parent company or division headquarters who would be most familiar with labor relations at all the company's plants. If your company is a single plant company, simply check here:

single plant company _____

Top labor relations executive: parent headquarters   _____
                                   division headquarters   _____

Name: _____
Title   _____
Address: _____

_____

_____

_____

Phone: _____

Finally: please enclose a copy of your current labor agreement.

Name of Respondent: _____

Company of Respondent: _____

Thank you again for responding to this questionnaire. As soon as the results have been compiled and analyzed, I will send you a copy of the key findings.

Appendix B

UNION LEADER SURVEY
Survey of Local Unions:
Joint Labor-Management Relations
Project

Union-management cooperative programs as defined for present purposes refer to activities **undertaken jointly** between companies and unions. The focus of such programs may be on company performance (for example, productivity committees or quality control circles), and/or worker satisfaction and well being (for example, quality of work life, employee involvement, and safety and health). Activities may also entail some form of incentive arrangement to increase company profitability and employee compensation (for example, Scanlon or Rucker gainsharing plans and profit sharing that include activities designed to increase employee involvement).

If you have **never** established any such joint programs, please complete sections I, II, and VI. If you **have** established any such program, even if it has not been fully implemented or has been terminated, please complete all sections of this questionnaire.

Lastly, questions that refer to **this company** or **this plant** pertain to the bargaining unit employees represented by your local union at the plant of the **company identified in the cover letter.**

SECTION I. Program Identification

Below is a table that identifies several kinds of programs. Under the various stages of the process identified at the top of the table, please provide the approximate months and year for each of the applicable stages.

167

Even if you have **not** established any kind of joint program, please indicate under column 1 if the establishment of **any kind of joint program** was given serious initial consideration, and if so, when.

Joint Program/Activity	Considered but Decided Against		Oversight or Steering Committee Established		Program Activities Began		Program Activity Became Widespread		Program Terminated	
	Month	Year	Month	Year	Month	Year	Month	Year	Month	Year
1. Quality of Work Life										
2. Productivity Committee										
3. Quality Control Circles										
4. Work Teams										
5. Training Committee										
6. Industrial Relations Com. (general problem solving)										
7. Scanlon Plan										
8. Rucker Plan										
9. Other Gainsharing Plan										
10. Health and Safety Comm.										
11. Substance Abuse Comm.										
12. ESOP (with employee involvement activities)										
13. Profit Sharing (with employee involvement activities)										
14. Other?										

SECTION II. General Information about Union and Plant

1. What proportion of production workers are represented by your union in this plant? _____ %

2. Which of the following best describes the bargaining structure between your union and this company?

    a. **Master agreement** with more than one plant of this company, plus supplemental local agreements at each plant. _____
    b. **Single-plant** agreement between your local and this plant. _____
    c. **Multi-employer** agreement between your union and more than one company. _____
    d. **Multi-union** agreement between one or more additional unions and this company. _____

3. Do you have a union-shop security clause in your agreement with this company?

    _____ Yes   _____ No

4. Do representatives from the national or regional union offices actively participate in your contract negotiations?

    _____ Yes   _____ No

5. Does the national union require national union approval of contracts negotiated by your local?

    _____ Yes   _____ No

6. Does your **local** union represent employees at **other** companies in your area?

    _____ Yes   _____ No

    If yes, how many other companies? _____

7. In what year did your union negotiate its first agreement with this company at your plant? _____

8. Is the top local officer elected by the local membership or is he or she an appointed business agent?

    _____ elected by local membership   _____ appointed business agent

9. How long has the current top local officer been in his/her position?

    _____ Years

10. What is the average length of employment within the bargaining unit?

    _____ Years

11. What proportion of the bargaining unit employees are female? _____ %

12. Since 1975, would you characterize any round of negotiations with this company as "concession" bargaining (where, for example, wages or benefits were frozen or cut or protective work rules were modified)?

    _____ Yes _____ No

    If **yes**, in what year or years were such concessions negotiated?

    _____   _____   _____

13. To what extent does the local union leadership **trust** management's capabilities to manage this company?

    _____ Very little   _____ Much
    _____ Little   _____ Very much

14. To what extent does this company treat the union as having a legitimate right to represent workers?

    _____ Very little right _____ Little right
    _____ Full right

15. Which of the following best describes the **overall relationship** between the bargaining unit and local management?

_____ Very good   _____ Poor

_____ Satisfactory   _____ Very poor

16. Is there an Area-Wide Joint Labor-Management Committee in your locality?

_____ Yes   _____ No   _____ Don't know

17. Is there an Industry-Wide Joint Labor-Management Committee in your industry?

_____ Yes   _____ No   _____ Don't know

18. To what extend do the following parties support the establishment of **joint** labor-management programs?

Party	Generally Opposed	Neutral	Generally in Favor
Local Union Leaders	_____	_____	_____
National Union Leaders	_____	_____	_____
Local Union Members	_____	_____	_____
Plant Management	_____	_____	_____
Company Executives	_____	_____	_____

SECTION III. Structure and Focus of Program Activities

A. Including any joint program that may have been terminated, please briefly describe the focus and structure of the joint effort that you consider to be the most important to union objectives (excluding health and safety activities).

1. **Key problem(s)** that led to and is addressed by program (for example, quality of work life, job security, low productivity, etc.):

_____

_____

_____

_____

2. **Kind of joint activities** (for example, work team arrange-
    ments, ad hoc tasks groups, regular meetings for employee
    input, etc.):

_____

_____

_____

_____

B. In reference to the program identified above, please answer the
    following questions.

    1. What proportion of bargaining unit employees are covered
        by the program?

        _____ %

    2. How frequent are meetings held by:

        (a) the highest level steering committee?

             every _____ weeks

        (b) the shop floor work groups or teams (if applicable)?

             every _____ weeks

    3. Are these meetings well attended by committee or team
        members? (please check)

	Very Well Attended	Well Attended	Poorly Attended
(a) Steering Committee Meetings	_____	_____	_____
(b) Shop Floor Committee Meetings	_____	_____	_____

4. How many union and company representatives sit on the highest level steering committee?

_____ # union rep.   _____ # company rep.

5. Who first promoted the development of the joint program?

_____ union   _____ company   _____ both union and company

C. Have any union representatives been assigned or elected by the union to act as joint program coordinators or facilitators?

_____ Yes   _____ No

If **yes**, how many union representatives are full-time or part-time coordinators or facilitators?

_____ # full-time   _____ # part-time

D. To what extent are joint labor-management activities allowed to modify either work rules or wages and benefits negotiated in the labor agreement? (please check)

	Not at all	Very little	Little	Much
Work rules	____	____	____	____
Wages and benefits	____	____	____	____

If work rules and/or wages and benefits can be modified through joint activities, what procedure or rules are followed in making modifications? (please briefly describe)

_____

_____

_____

_____

E. To what extent do union representatives who serve on the contract negotiation team or who are regular grievance committeemen also serve in key positions in joint labor-management committees?

_____ Not at all   _____ Much overlap

_____ Very little overlap   _____ Very much overlap

F. Has the national or regional union office provided expertise or resources to your local for joint labor-management activities?

_____ Yes _____ No

G. Has any neutral outside consultant(s) been used to help facilitate your joint efforts?

_____ Yes _____ No

H. To what extent have tradeoffs been made between promotion of the union's **social** concerns or objectives (for example, concerns for older workers, minorities, females, safety and health, etc.) and joint labor-management program objectives?

Considerable tradeoff _____   Some tradeoff _____

Little or no tradeoff _____

I. To what extent has your plant worked with the following organizations in designing and/or implementing cooperative programs?

Organization	Not at all	Some	Very Much
Area-Wide Joint Labor-Management Committee	_____	_____	_____
Industry-Wide Joint Labor-Management Committee	_____	_____	_____
Federal Mediation & Concilliation Service (FMCS)	_____	_____	_____
U.S. Department of Labor	_____	_____	_____

SECTION IV. Comparison of Conditions Before and After Joint Program Implementation

Comparing the five year period prior to implementation of the most important joint program identified above, please indicate the degree to which the variables identified below have changed.

Extent of Change

Variable	Much Higher	Modestly Higher	About the Same	Modestly Lower	Much Lower
1. Union member satisfaction with job tasks.	_____	_____	_____	_____	_____
2. Level of job security.	_____	_____	_____	_____	_____
3. Work conditions and quality of work life.	_____	_____	_____	_____	_____
4. Sharing of information by management.	_____	_____	_____	_____	_____
5. Management understanding of worker interests and problems.	_____	_____	_____	_____	_____
6. Management understanding of union role, interests, and objectives.	_____	_____	_____	_____	_____

7. Union leaders' understanding of management's business interests and problems. _____ _____ _____ _____ _____

8. Union members' understanding of management's business interests and problems. _____ _____ _____ _____ _____

9. Joint problem solving relationship between union leaders and managers. _____ _____ _____ _____ _____

10. Union input into business decisions. _____ _____ _____ _____ _____

11. Cooperative spirit in contract negotiations. _____ _____ _____ _____ _____

12. Problem solving relationship between supervisors and union members. _____ _____ _____ _____ _____

13. Union's ability to resolve member grievances or problems satisfactorily. _____ _____ _____ _____ _____

14. Union member commitment to union _____ _____ _____ _____ _____

15. Union member commitment to company. _____ _____ _____ _____ _____

16. Public image of union. _____ _____ _____ _____ _____

17. Worker productivity. _____ _____ _____ _____ _____

18. Product quality. _____ _____ _____ _____ _____

19. Level of scrappage or waste. _____ _____ _____ _____ _____

20. Rate of grievances. _____ _____ _____ _____ _____

21. Rate of absenteeism/tardiness. _____ _____ _____ _____ _____

22. Flexibility of work rules. _____ _____ _____ _____ _____

23. Other variables?

_____ _____ _____ _____ _____ _____

SECTION V. Problems in Implementing and Maintaining Joint Program Activities

Problems obviously arise as joint program activities are implemented. To what extent have the following problems affected the successful implementation and maintenance of your most important joint program, identified above?

Extent of Problem

Potential Problems	Not a Problem	Somewhat a Problem	Very much a Problem	Important Factor in Termination of Program
1. Lack of experience or expertise in devising and implementing joint programs.	_____	_____	_____	_____
2. Lack of sufficient trust between parties.	_____	_____	_____	_____
3. Violation of trust by either party.	_____	_____	_____	_____
4. Lack of adequate preparation of plant management for change.	_____	_____	_____	_____
5. Lack of adequate orientation and training for bargaining unit employees for change.	_____	_____	_____	_____
6. Lack of commitment by upper management.	_____	_____	_____	_____
7. Lack of broad commitment among plant managers.	_____	_____	_____	_____
8. Turnover of key managers.	_____	_____	_____	_____
9. Lack of broad commitment by union leaders.	_____	_____	_____	_____
10. Turnover of key union leaders.	_____	_____	_____	_____
11. Skepticism or lack of interest by workers.	_____	_____	_____	_____
12. Balancing joint activities and contract negotiations	_____	_____	_____	_____
13. Balancing joint activities and contract administration (e.g. grievance handling).	_____	_____	_____	_____
14. Perceived manipulation of program (or bonus formula) by management.	_____	_____	_____	_____
15. Perception by workers that union leadership has been coopted by management.	_____	_____	_____	_____
16. Insufficient job security.	_____	_____	_____	_____

17. Continued reduction in work
     force.   _____ _____ _____ _____

18. Expected gains from program not
     gotten.   _____ _____ _____ _____

Other than the potential problems identified above, please briefly describe other problems that you have encountered and/or elaborate, if you wish on any of potential problems identified above.

_____

_____

_____

_____

SECTION VI.   **Thank you** again for responding to this questionnaire. As soon as the results have been compiled and analyzed, I will send you a summary of the key findings.

Name of Respondent: _____

Name of Union: _____

Phone number: _____

Lastly, as part of the analysis, it would be very helpful to have a copy of your current labor agreement. Therefore, we ask that you please enclose a copy of your agreement.

HEADQUARTERS EXECUTIVE SURVEY
Management-Union Cooperation Research Project

A. Company Structure

1. At what operating level are key strategic decisions made regarding manufacturing operations (i.e., major capital investments, acquisitions, plant closure, etc.)?

_____ parent   _____ subsidiary
headquarters   headquarters

_____ operating   _____ division
headquarters   headquarters

2. At what operating level are key strategic policies made regarding labor-management relations (i.e., key negotiation issues, union avoidance, joint management-union activities, etc.)?

_____ parent   _____ subsidiary
headquarters   headquarters

_____ operating   _____ division
headquarters   headquarters

3. If you represent a subsidiary, operating company, or division of a parent company, please complete a, b, c, and d below.

(a) Name of Parent Co.: _____
Address: _____
_____
_____

(b) Top labor relations executive at parent headquarters.

179

Name: _____

Phone: _____

(c) Name of subsidiary, operating company, or division headquarters that you represent:

Name of Organization: _____

_____ subsidiary _____ operating co.

_____ division

(d) By drawing arrows between the organizational units below, indicate the linkages between your subsidary, operating company or divison and the parent company:

```
┌─────────────────────────────────────────────┐
│                   Parent Co.                  │
│                                               │
│                                               │
│  Subsidiary                      Operating Co. │
│                                               │
│                                               │
│                    Division                   │
└─────────────────────────────────────────────┘
```

Please answer the questions below as they apply to your level within the organization structure (parent company, subsidiary, etc.).

These data are for statistical purposes only. All answers will remain confidential.

B. Manufacturing Facilities

1. How many domestic manufacturing plants are there within the company?

_____ # of unionized facilities   _____ # of non-union facilities

2. Since 1975, how many domestic manufacturing plants have been opened or acquired and are still in operation?

_____ # of unionized plants   _____ # of non-union plants

3. Since 1975, how many domestic manufacturing plants have been permanently shut down?

_____ # of unionized plants   _____ # of non-union plants

4. How many unionized domestic manufacturing plants have some formalized joint management-union activities designed to improve company performance and/or quality of work life? _____

5. How many manufacturing plants are located outside of North America? _____

6. Approximately what proportion of total manufacturing production is produced outside North America? _____ % total production.

7. Approximately what proportion of total manufacturing products (components and finished goods) are sold outside North America? _____ % total worldwide sales.

8. Since 1975, have there been any major changes in company structure due to merger with other companies, major acquisitions, or joint ventures? Yes _____   No _____

If yes, please briefly identify these mergers, acquisitions, or joint ventures.

_____

_____

_____

_____

C. Company Policy In Unionized Facilities

1. In general, company executives are

_____ not in favor of   _____ in favor of
_____ indifferent to **joint** management-union programs or activities.

2. Specifically, the company has: (check one)

_____ a. instructed plant management to actively pursue **joint** management-union activities.

_____ b. instructed management **NOT** to engage in **joint** management-union activities.

_____ c. left the decision to engage in **joint** management-union activities to plant level managers.

3. To what extent are top union officers involved in **strategic** management decisions affecting your manufacturing operations?

_____ very much involved _____ somewhat involved

_____ much involved   _____ not involved

Please briefly describe any such involvement.   _____

_____

_____

_____

4. In general, it is company policy to:

_____ strongly oppose _____ oppose
_____ remain neutral to union representation of non-union manufacturing plants.

5. How many union organizing drives have occurred in the last 5 years at your manufacturing plants?

_____ # of successful union organizing drives
_____ # of unsuccessful union organizing drives

6. Have there been any union **decertification** efforts in the last 5 years at your manufacturing plant?

Yes _____   No _____

If yes, how many?

_____ # of decertification drives unions have lost

_____ # of decertification drives unions have won

Thank you again for your assistance.

D. Respondent

Name: _____

Title: _____

Company: _____

Address: _____

             _____

Phone: _____

References

Amemiya, Takeshi. "Qualitative Response Models: A Survey," *Journal of Economic Literature*, Vol. 19, December 1981, 1483-1536.

Banks, Andy and Jack Metzgar. "Participating in Management: Union Organizing on a New Terrain," *Labor Research Review*, Vol. 8, No. 2, Fall 1989, 5-55.

Barbash, Jack. *The Elements of Industrial Relations*, Madison: University of Wisconsin Press, 1984.

Bieber, Owen. "UAW Views Circles: Not Bad at All," *Labor-Management Cooperation: Perspectives From the Labor Movement*, U.S. Department of Labor, Bureau of Labor-Management Relations and Cooperative Programs, 1984, 34.

Bluestone, Irving. "Joint Action: The New Track of Labor-Management Relations," *Workplace Democracy*, No. 56, Spring 1987: 14-15, 25.

Boyle, Fosten A. "An Evolving Process of Participation: Honeywell and Teamsters Local 1145," in Jerome M. Rosow, editor *Teamwork*, New York: Pergamon Press, 1986, 146-168.

Boylston, Benjamin C. "Employee Involvement and Cultural Change at Bethlehem Steel," in Jerome M. Rosow, editor *Teamwork*, New York: Pergamon Press, 1986, 89-109.

Burck, Charles G. "Working Smarter," *Fortune*, June 1981(a), 68-73.

Burck, Charles G. "What's in It for the Unions?" *Fortune*, August 24, 1981(b), 88-92.

Camens, Sam. "Labor-Management Participation Teams in the Basic Steel Industry," in Jerome M. Rosow, editor, *Teamwork*, New York: Pergamon Press, 1986, 110-118.

Cammann, Cortlandt, Edward E. Lawler III, Gerald E. Ledford, and Stanley E. Seashore. *Management-Labor Cooperation in Quality of Worklife Experiments: Comparative Analysis of Eight Cases*, a technical report to the U.S. Department of Labor, University of Michigan, 1984.

Chamberlain, Neil W. *Collective Bargaining*, New York: McGraw Hill, 1951.

Cohen-Rosenthal, Edward and Cynthia E. Burton. *Mutual Gains*, New York: Praeger, 1987.

Contino, Ronald. "Productivity Gains Through Labor-Management Cooperation at the N.Y.C. Department of Sanitation Bureau of Motor Equipment," in Jerome M. Rosow, editor *Teamwork*, New York: Pergamon Press, 1986, 169-186.

Cooke, William N. "Toward a General Theory of Industrial Relations," in David B. Lipsky, editor, *Advances in Industrial and Labor Relations*, Vol. 2, Greenwich, CT:JAI Press, 1985, 233-252.

Cooke, William N. and David G. Meyer. "Structural and Market Predictors of Corporate Labor Relations Strategies," *Industrial and Labor Relations Review*, Vol. 43, No. 2, January 1990, 280-293.

Cooke, William N. (a) "Improving Productivity and Quality Through Collaboration," *Industrial Relations*, Vol. 28, No.2, Spring 1989, 299-319.

Cooke, William N. (b) "Cooperative Efforts to Solve Employment Problems," *Investing in People: A Strategy to Address America's Workforce Crises*, Vol. 2, Commission on Workforce Quality and Labor Market Efficiency, U.S. Department of Labor, September 1989, 2057-2130.

Cooke, William N. "Factors Influencing the Effect of Joint Union-Management Programs on Employee-Supervisor Relations," *Industrial and Labor Relations Review*, Vol. 43, No. 5, July 1990, 587-603.

Cummings, Thomas G. and Edmond S. Molloy. *Improving Productivity and the Quality of Work Life*, New York: Praeger, 1977.

Cutcher-Gershenfeld, Joel. *The Case of Xerox Corporation and the Amalgamated Clothing and Textile Workers Union*," U.S. Department of Labor, BLMR 123, 1988.

Delaney, John T., Casey Ichniowski, and David Lewin. "Employee Involvement Programs and Firm Performance," Proceedings of the 41st IRRA, 1988.

de Schweinitz, Dorothea. *Labor and Management in Common Enterprise*. Cambridge: Harvard University Press, 1949.

Douty, Harry. *Labor-Management Productivity Committees in American Industry*, Washington, D.C.: National Commission on Productivity and Work Quality, 1975.

Driscoll, James W. "Labor-Management Panels: Three Case Studies," *Monthly Labor Review* Vol. 103, No. 6, June 1980, 41-44.

Dulworth, Michael. "Employee Involvement and Gainsharing Produce Results at Eggers Industries," *Labor-Management Cooperation Brief*, U.S. Department of Labor, Bureau of Labor-Management Relations and Cooperative Programs, March 1985.

Dyer, Lee, David B. Lipsky and Thomas Kochan. "Union Attitudes Toward Management Cooperation," *Industrial Relations*, Vol. 16, No. 2, May 1977, 163-172.

Dunlop, John T. *Industrial Relations Systems*. New York: Holt, Rinehart, and Winston, 1958.

Dunlop, John T. "A Decade of National Experience," in Jerome M. Rosow, editor, *Teamwork*, New York: Pergamon Press, 1986, 12-25.

Ephlin, Donald F. "United Auto Workers: Pioneers in Labor-Management Partnership," in Jerome M. Rosow, editor, *Teamwork*, New York: Pergamon Press, 1986, 133-145.

Fraser, Douglas A. "A Labor Director Looks at the Board," in Jerome M. Rosow, editor *Teamwork*, New York: Pergamon Press, 1986, 56-72.

Freedman, Audrey. *Managing Labor Relations*, New York: The Conference Board, 1979.

Freedman, Audrey. *The New Look in Wage Bargaining*, New York: The Conference Board, 1985.

Fuller, Steven H. "Employee Participation for Productivity: A Management View," in Jerome M. Rosow, editor, *Productivity: Prospects for Growth*, New York: Van Nostrand Reinhold, 1981, 296-309.

Goodman, Paul S. "Realities of Improving the Quality of Work Life: Quality-of-Work Life Projects in the 1980s," in *Proceedings of the 1980 Spring Meeting*, Industrial Relations Research Association, Madison, Wis., 1980, 487-494.

Goodman, Paul S. and Edward E. Lawler, III. "United States," in *New Forms of Work Organization*, 1, Geneva: International Labour Organization, 1979, 141-173.

Greenberg, Paul and Edward Glaser. *Some Issues in Joint Union Management Quality of Work Life Improvement Efforts*, Kalamazoo, MI: Upjohn Institute, 1980.

Guest, Robert H. "Quality of Work Life—Learning from Tarrytown," *Harvard Business Review*, Vol. 57, No. 4, July-August 1979, 76-87.

Hammer, Tove H. and Robert N. Stern. "A Yo-Yo Model of Cooperation: Union Participation in Management at the Rath Packing Company," *Industrial and Labor Relations Review*, Vol. 39, No. 3, April 1986, 337-349.

Hoyer, Denise T. and Gregory E. Huszczo. *Forging Partnership Through Employee Involvement*, U.S. Department of Labor, BLMR 130, 1988.

IAM Research Report. *Labor Management Cooperation: Perspectives From The Labor Movement*, U.S. Department of Labor, Bureau of Labor-Management Relations and Cooperative Programs, 1984, 16-21.

Jacoby, Sanford. "Union-Management Cooperation in the United States: Lessons from the 1920's," *Industrial and Labor Relations Review*, Vol. 37, No. 1, October 1983, 18-33.

Jick, Todd D., Robert B. McKersie, Leonard Greenblaugh. "A Process Analysis of Labor-Management Committee Problem Solving," *Proceedings of the 1982 Annual Meeting*, Industrial Relations Research Association, Madison, WIS., 1982, 182-188.

Katz, Harry C., Thomas A. Kochan, and Kenneth R. Gobeille. "Industrial Relations Performance, Economic Performance, and QWL Programs: An Interplant Analysis," *Industrial and Labor Relations Review*, Vol. 37, No. 1, October 1983, 3-17.

Katz, Harry C., Thomas A. Kochan, and Mark Weber. "Assessing the Effects of Industrial Relations and Quality of Working Life Efforts on Organizational Effectiveness," *Academy of Management Journal*, Vol. 28, September 1985, 509-526.

Katz, Harry C., Thomas A. Kochan, and Jeffrey H. Keefe. "Industrial Relations and Productivity in the U.S. Automobile Industry," *Brookings Papers on Economic Activity*, Vol. 3, 1987, 685-715.

Kochan, Thomas A., Harry C. Katz, and Nancy R. Mower. *Worker Participation and American Unions*, Kalamazoo, MI: Upjohn Institute, 1984.

Kochan, Thomas A., and Lee Dyer. "A Model of Organizational Change in the Context of Union-Management Relations," *The Journal of Applied Behavioral Science*, Vol. 12, No. 1, January-February-March 1976, 59-78.

Kochan, Thomas A., Robert B. McKersie, and Peter Cappelli. "Strategic Choice and Industrial Relations Theory," *Industrial Relations*, Vol. 23, No. 1, Winter 1984, 16-39.

Kochan, Thomas A., Robert B. McKersie, and John Chalykoff. "The Effects of Corporate Strategy and Workplace Innovations on Union Representation," *Industrial and Labor Relations Review*, Vol. 39, No. 4, July 1986, 487-501.

Kochan, Thomas A., Harry C. Katz, and Robert B. McKersie. *The Transformation of American Industrial Relations*, New York: Basic Books, Inc., 1986.

Kochan, Thomas A. and Joel Cutcher-Gershenfeld. "Institutionizing and Diffusing Innovations in Industrial Relations," U.S. Department of Labor, BLMR 128, 1988.

Lawler, Edward, E. III, and John A. Drexler, Jr. "Dynamics of Establishing Cooperative Quality of Work Life Projects," *Monthly Labor Review*, 101, March 1978, 23-28.

Lazes, Peter and Tony Costanza. "Xerox Cuts Costs Without Layoffs Through Union-Management Collaboration," *Labor-Management Cooperation Brief*, U.S. Department of Labor, Bureau of Labor-Management Relations and Cooperative Programs, July 1984.

Lee, Barbara. "The Ethicon/ACTWU Work Involvement Process," U.S. Department of Labor, BLMR III, 1987.

Levine, David I. and George Strauss. "Employee Participation and Involvement," *Investing in People: A Strategy to Address America's Workforce Crises*, Vol. 2, Commission on Workforce Quality and Labor Market Efficiency, U.S. Department of Labor, September 1989, 1893-1948.

McIntosh, Phyllis L. "Labor Compact Key to New Employee-Management Partnership at Dayton Power and Light," U.S. Department of Labor, *Brief*, No. 12, January 1988.

Meyer, David G. and William N. Cooke. "Economic and Political Factors in Formal Grievance Resolution," *Industrial Relations*, 27, 3, Fall 1988, 318-325.

Meyer, David G. and William N. Cooke. "Labor Relations in Transition: Strategy Implementation and Effects on Financial Performance," working paper, 1990.

Oswald, Rudolph A. "Joint Labor-Management Programs," in Jerome M. Rosow, editor, *Teamwork*, New York: Pergamon Press, 1986, 26-40.

Parker, Mike. *Inside the Circle: A Union Guide to QWL*, Boston: South End Press, 1985.

Pearlstein, Gloria. "Preston Trucking Drives for Productivity," U.S. Department of Labor, *Brief*, No. 13, February 1988.

Roadley, Thomas H., "Riding the Road to Recovery at Harley-Davidson," U.S. Department of Labor, *Brief*, No. 15, April 1988.

Rosenberg, Richard D. and Eliezer Rosenstein. "Participation and Productivity: An Empirical Study," *Industrial and Labor Relations Review*, Vol. 33, No. 3, April 1980, 355-361.

Rosow, Jerome M. "Quality of Work Life Issues for the 1980's," in Clark Kerr and Jerome Rosow, editors, *Work in America: The Decade Ahead*, New York: Van Nostrand Reinhold, Co., 1979, 157-187.

Rosow, Jerome M. "Teamwork: Pros, Cons, and Prospects for the Future," in Rosow, editor, *Teamwork*, New York: Pergamon Press, 1986.

Ross, Timothy L. and Ruth Ann Ross. "Dana's Hyco Plant Successfully Integrates Quality Circles and Gainsharing," U.S. Department of Labor, *Brief*, No. 7, July 1986.

Ruttenberg, Ruth. "The Role of Labor-Management Committees in Safeguarding Worker Safety and Health," U.S. Department of Labor, BLMR 121, 1988.

Schlesinger, Leonard A. and Richard E. Walton. "The Process of Work Restructuring and Its Impact on Collective Bargaining," *Monthly Labor Review*, 100, 4, April 1977, 52-55.

Schuster, Michael H. *Union-Management Cooperation*, Kalamazoo, MI: Upjohn Institute, 1984.

Schuster, Michael H. "The Impact of Union-Management Cooperation on

Productivity and Employment," *Industrial and Labor Relations Review*, Vol. 36, No. 3, April 1983, 415-430.

Schuster, Michael H. "Innovative Compensation Systems: Implications for Employers, Unions, and Government," *Investing in People: A Strategy to Address America's Workforce Crises*, Vol. 2, Commission on Workforce Quality and Labor Market Efficiency, U.S. Department of Labor, September 1989, 1727-1774.

Siegel, Irving H., and Edgar Weinberg. *Labor-Management Cooperation: The American Experience*, Kalamazoo, MI: Upjohn Institute, 1982.

Simmons, John and William Mares. *Working Together*, New York: New York University Press, 1985.

Slichter, Sumner H. *Union Policies and Industrial Management*, Washington, D.C.: The Brookings Institution, 1941.

Slichter, Sumner H., James J. Healy, and E. Robert Livernash. *The Impact of Collective Bargaining on Management*, Washington, D.C.: The Brookings Institution, 1960.

Smaby, Beverly, Christopher Meek, Catherine Barnes, Joseph Blasi, and Preeta Bansal. "Labor-Management Cooperation at Eastern Airlines," U.S. Department of Labor, BLMR 118, 1988.

Smith, Michal. (a) "Employee Involvement Fuels Dramatic Turnaround at Ford's Louisville Assembly Plant," U.S. Department of Labor, *Brief*, No. 9, November 1986.

Smith, Michal. (b) "Aladdin's Magic," U.S. Department of Labor, *Brief*, No. 12, January 1988.

Spector, Paul E. "Perceived Control by Employees: A Meta-Analysis of Studies Concerning Autonomy and Participation at Work," *Human Relations*, Vol. 39, No. 11, November 1986, 1005-1016.

Strauss, George. "Quality of Worklife and Participation as Bargaining Issues," in Harvey Juris and Myron Roomkin, editors, *The Shrinking Perimeter*, Lexington, MA: Lexington Books, 1980.

Thompson, Philip C. "Quality Circles at Martin Marietta Corporation, Denver Aerospace/Michoud Division," *The Innovative Organization*, New York: Pergamon Press, 1982, 3-20.

UBC Bulletin, *Labor-Management Cooperation: Perspectives From The Labor Movement*, U.S. Department of Labor, Bureau of Labor-Management Relations and Cooperative Programs, 1984, 39-43.

U.S. Department of Labor. Labor-Management Services Administration, *Report of the Secretary of Labor's Symposium on Cooperative Labor-Management Programs*, Washington, D.C., 1982.

U.S. Department of Labor. Labor-Management Services Administration, *Re-

port of the Secretary of Labor's Southeast Regional Symposium on Cooperative Labor-Management Programs, Washington, D.C., 1983.

Verma, Anil. "Relative Flow of Capital to Union and Nonunion Plants Within a Firm," *Industrial Relations*, Vol. 24, No. 3, Fall 1985, 395-405.

Verma, Anil and Robert B. McKersie. "Employee Involvement: The Implications of Noninvolvement by Unions," *Industrial and Labor Relations Review*, Vol. 40, No. 4, July 1987, 556-568.

Voos, Paula B. "The Influence of Cooperative Programs on Union-Management Relations, Flexibility, and Other Labor Relations Outcomes," *Journal of Labor Research*, Vol. 10, No. 1, Winter 1989, 103-117.

Voos, Paula B. "Managerial Perceptions of the Economic Impact of Labor Relations Programs," *Industrial and Labor Relations Review*, Vol. 40, No. 2, January 1987, 195-208.

Walton, Richard E. and Robert B. McKersie. *A Behavioral Theory of Labor Negotiations*, New York: McGraw-Hill, 1965.

Walton, Richard E. "From Control to Commitment in the Workplace," *Harvard Business Review*, March-April, 1985.

Watts, Glen. "Quality of Work Life," *Perspective*, Labor Relations Press, October 1982.

Wever, Kirsten R. *Western Airlines and Its Four Major Unions*, U.S. Department of Labor, BLMR 129, 1988.

Wintergreen Symposium Report. U.S. Department of Labor, BLMR 101, 1986.

Work in America Institute, Inc. *Productivity Through Work Innovations*, New York: Pergamon Press, 1982.

Whyte, William F., Tove H. Hammer, Christopher Meek, Reed Nelson, and Robert N. Stern. *Worker Participation and Ownership*, Ithaca: ILR Press, 1983.

Index

Absenteeism/tardiness, 82
Adversarial relationship, labor-management, 85
Amemiya, Takeshi, 55
Arbitration, 26

Banks, Andy, 11
Barbash, Jack, 19
Bargaining skill, 26-27
Benefits: from joint effort, 40-41
Benefits of cooperation: intrinsic and extrinsic nature of, 37-38; for management and labor of, 6-8, 9-13; with power options, 35-37
Bieber, Owen, 13
Bluestone, Irving, 16
Boyle, Fosten A., 7, 8, 10, 97
Boylston, Benjamin C., 7, 53
Burck, Charles G., 8, 10, 12, 13
Burton, Cynthia E., 7, 8, 13, 14

Camens, Sam, 7, 11, 15
Cammann, Cortlandt, 5, 8, 12
Capacity: human, 27; technical, 28
Capelli, Peter, 75n111
Chalykoff, John, 4, 47-48
Chamberlain, Neil W., 23-25
Cohen-Rosenthal, Edward, 7, 8, 13, 14
Collective bargaining: balanced with cooperative efforts, 16, 32, 133-36; challenge to, 1
Commitment: in cooperative efforts, 15; correlation with trust of, 131-32; level in joint programs of, 125-32; with use of relative power, 135; *See also* Distrust; Trust
Compensation, 150-52
Competition, global, 45
Conflict of interest, 22, 32
Contino, Ronald, 7
Cooke, William N., 19, 20, 27, 48, 52, 96, 105, 107-8
Cooperation, labor-management: as selling point for unions, 139-40; sharing of gains in, 21, 32-33, 40, 145-53
Cooperation strategy: estimation of factors influencing choice of, 55-57, 72-72; in Headquarters Executive Survey, 51-53; joint cooperative programs for, 61-63, 72, 154; measurement of choices for, 57-61; to reduce union membership, 46-47
Cooperative activities: problems of, 14-16
Cooperative activities, committee-based, 64, 66, 68, 73-74, 154; hypothetical structure and outcome for, 96
Cooperative activities, labor-management, 5; benefit and cost potential of, 6-14; commitment to programs of, 125-32; determinants of choice of, 65-66; effects across establishments of, 90-93; focus and structure of, 64-73; gain sharing in, 150-52; initiation and establishment of, 61-63, 66-67; intensity level of, 94-95; juxtaposed with contract negotiation and administration, 134-35; model to test success of, 93-105; net gains perceived, 40; outcome perceived, 34-35, 81-90;

Mares, William, 9, 11, 13
Metzgar, Jack, 11
Meyer, David G., 27, 48, 52, 105, 107-8
Milwaukee Spring Division of Illinois Coil Spring Company v. *UAW Local 547*, 41n2
Mixed strategy: factors influencing choice of, 55-57, 72-73; in Headquarters Executive Survey, 50-53; joint cooperative programs for, 61-63, 72; measurement of choices for, 57-61; to reduce union membership, 46-47
Models, 22-25, 93-105, 114-15, 118-19
Molloy, Edmond S., 10
Mower, Nancy R., 8, 10, 13, 14, 15

Negotiation: concession or give-back, 30, 32; skill in, 26-27
Nonunion competition, 1, 44-45

Oswald, Rudolph A., 11, 53
Outcomes: demoralizing, 132-33; perceptions of, 35, 81-90; primary and secondary variables for, 37-38
Parker, Mike, 10
Pearlstein, Gloria, 7, 10
Perception: of cooperation, 29, 145; of costs and benefits, 52-54; of gains, 88; of outcomes, 35, 81-90; of understanding, 85
Plant count, companywide, 57
Plant Manager Survey: analysis of, 61-62; data base for, 48-49; focus an structure of joint programs in, 64; questionnaire for, 157-66; response to issue of trust and commitment in, 122-25, 132
Power, relative: achieving balance in cooperative activity for, 98-99; in collective bargaining, 145; definition and model of, 22-25; management choice based on, 52; management options for achieving, 39-41; for maximizing utility, 29, 93, 135; to obtain absolute utility, 40-41; reinforcement of, 38-39; role in joint cooperative efforts of, 138-39; sources of, 25-26; used with cooperation, 134-35; use in conflict of interest issues, 32
Power, total, 22-23
Power, total organizational: definition and components of, 27-28; for maximizing utility, 29-30, 93
Productivity, 90-91
Productivity Committees, 64
Profit-sharing programs, cooperative, 62-63

Quality circle program, 24, 62, 64
Quality of Work Life (QWL), 3-4, 64, 91-92

Roadley, Thomas H., 7
Rosenberg, Richard D., 7
Rosenstein, Eliezer, 7
Rosow, Jerome M., 9, 15
Ross, Ruth Ann, 10
Ross, Timothy L., 10
Rules, formal and informal, 26
Rules, work: effect of joint cooperative programs on, 71; flexibility with cooperation, 82

198

Utility, relative, 30, 32
Utility, total, 22; maximization of, 27, 30; potential to increase, 38-39

Verma, Anil, 8, 75n11
Voos, Paula B., 4, 7, 16, 91

Wages, 71
Walton, Richard E., 8, 9, 14, 32
Watts, Glen, 8, 13, 14
Weber, Mark, 7, 16, 92
Weinberg, Edgar, 8, 9
Wever, Kirsten, 16
Wintergreen Symposium Report, 15
Work in America Institute, Inc., 10, 11, 13, 14